MAKING A DIFFERENCE

MAKING A DIFFERENCE

Fifty years of Indigenous Programs at Monash University, 1964–2014

RANI KERIN

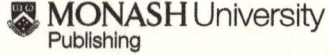

© Copyright 2016 Rani Kerin
All rights reserved. Apart from any uses permitted by Australia's Copyright Act 1968, no part of this book may be reproduced by any process without prior written permission from the copyright owners. Inquiries should be directed to the publisher.

Monash University Publishing
Matheson Library and Information Services Building
40 Exhibition Walk
Monash University
Clayton, Victoria 3800, Australia
www.publishing.monash.edu

Monash University Publishing brings to the world publications which advance the best traditions of humane and enlightened thought.

Monash University Publishing titles pass through a rigorous process of independent peer review.

www.publishing.monash.edu/books/md-9781925377248.html

Series: Indigenous Studies

Design: Les Thomas

Cover image: Monash Indigenous Centre's possum skin cloak, made by Loraine Padgham, Taungurung Language Group. The separate designs on each pelt represent the various disciplines taught at Monash University.

National Library of Australia Cataloguing-in-Publication entry:

Creator:	Kerin, Rani, author.
Title:	Making a difference : fifty years of Indigenous programs at Monash University, 1964 - 2014 / Rani Kerin.
ISBN:	9781925377248 (paperback)
Subjects:	Monash University. Centre for Research into Aboriginal Affairs--History.
	Aboriginal Australians--Education (Higher).
	Aboriginal Australians--Social conditions.
	Universities and colleges--Public services.
	Community and college--Australia.
Dewey Number:	378.00899915

Printed in Australia by Griffin Press an Accredited ISO AS/NZS 14001:2004 Environmental Management System printer.

The paper this book is printed on is certified against the Forest Stewardship Council ® Standards. Griffin Press holds FSC chain of custody certification SGS-COC-005088. FSC promotes environmentally responsible, socially beneficial and economically viable management of the world's forests.

CONTENTS

Acknowledgements vi
Introduction vii

Chapter 1
The Centre, 1964–70. 1

Chapter 2
Embedding and Expanding, 1971–76. 22

Chapter 3
Aboriginalisation, 1977–97. 43

Chapter 4
MOSA: Creating Opportunities. 80

Chapter 5
Rebuilding Potential, 1997–2014 119

Discussion of Sources 145
Index 149

This book contains the names and images of Aboriginal people now deceased.

ACKNOWLEDGEMENTS

I have incurred many debts in researching and writing this book. I extend my sincere and lasting thanks to Professor Merle Ricklefs, Dr Janice Newton, Dr Liz Reed, Dr Angela Risdale, Professor Colin Tatz AO, Professor Eve Fesl AM, Helen Bnads, Emeritus Professor Colin Bourke MBE, Associate Professor Eleanor Bourke, Rob Hyatt, Kerrie Keleher, Sue Stevenson, Emeritus Professor Louis Waller AO, Professor Lynette Russell AO, Jason Brailey, and Helen Fletcher-Kennedy, all of whom kindly agreed to be interviewed and gave generously of their time and memories; Aunty Diane Singh, Elder in Residence, who put me in contact with people to interview; and the staff of the Monash University Archives – Lyn Maloney, Jan Getson, Karen Rogers – whose good humour and friendly banter made working in the basement of Building 3D a distinct pleasure. I am also grateful for the wise counsel of the book's steering committee, Emeritus Professor Graeme Davison, Professor Lynette Russell, Emeritus Professor Colin Bourke, Professor Andrew Markus, and Jason Brailey; the helpful comments of my HDR students at Federation University who unwittingly acted as sounding boards as I tested out ideas and arguments; and the love, forgiveness and patience of my family and friends who didn't see very much of me for twelve months, especially Maeve, Saffron and Daniel. Finally, I wish to thank Professor Rae Frances, Dean of Arts, and the Eggleston Foundation whose munificence made everything possible.

INTRODUCTION

With the establishment of the Centre for Research into Aboriginal Affairs (CRAA) in 1964, Monash became the first university to support research and teaching about contemporary Aboriginal Australia. In subsequent years, with the establishment of the Monash Orientation Scheme for Aborigines (MOSA) and other initiatives, Monash was at the forefront of moves to widen educational and employment opportunities for Indigenous people. The CRAA's work, its purpose, as interpreted by Colin Bourke, Director from 1977 to 1981, was 'to undertake and stimulate research [into] … the problems Aborigines have in living in a predominantly white society *with the aim of helping [to] bring about an improvement in that situation*'. Whether consciously or not, the Centre's work was inherently political; inherently activist. In seeking to improve the material circumstances of Aboriginal people via research, it necessarily sought to change society. Now fifty years old and renamed the Monash Indigenous Centre, it, together with the Yulendj Indigenous Engagement Unit, continues to strive to make a difference in Aboriginal peoples' lives because there is still more work to be done, more improvements to be made, and better understandings to be reached.

Convinced that Monash's fifty-year engagement with indigenous issues was worth celebrating, and learning from, in 2014 the directors of MIC and Yulendj – Professor Lynette Russell and Helen Fletcher-Kennedy respectively – invited Graeme Davison, Emeritus Professor of History and co-author of *University Unlimited: The Monash Story*, to advise on the process of writing a history of Monash's Indigenous programs. Davison recommended that a committee be established and an historian commissioned. Initially conceived as a six-month part-time commission to write a 20,000 word manuscript, the project was later extended to twelve-months part-time and 40–50,000 words thanks to a generous donation from the Eggleston Foundation, matched by in-kind support from Monash University.

I was commissioned to write the history. A Monash history graduate, my background is in twentieth-century Aboriginal political history and biography. Knowing very little about the history of Monash's Indigenous programs, I approached the University Archives with mixed feelings of trepidation and excitement. Fletcher-Kennedy, in briefing me about the project, related an experience in the University Archives. She had accompanied a small group from Yulendj on a reconnaissance mission to try and get a feel for the nature and scope of the collection. An archivist had shown them a random file which contained a letter from a Catholic priest to someone involved in MOSA. Fletcher-Kennedy hadn't taken note of the author, its addressee, when it was written (though she thought early 1990s), or which file it was in, but she remembered the statement at the bottom of the letterhead: 'Don't study Aboriginal languages – If ENGLISH was good enough for Jesus, it is good enough for you'. For Fletcher-Kennedy and the team at Yulendj, the letter exemplified the entrenched racism that Monash's Indigenous programs had sought to shift. Unsure what I would find, but determined to find the letter, I commenced work in January 2015. I was thrilled to discover on my first day in the basement where the University Archives are housed a handwritten note from Charles Duguid to Louis Matheson, Monash's Vice Chancellor, congratulating him on the establishment

INTRODUCTION

of the CRAA. Duguid, a leading campaigner for Aboriginal rights, was the subject of my doctoral thesis; I felt right at home.

It took me six months to find the priest's letter. In the meantime a picture emerged of burgeoning academic and wider public interest in contemporary Aboriginal Affairs that was led by Monash researchers; of attitudinal shifts helped along by the teaching of 'Black Studies' by Aboriginal people at Monash; of increasing numbers of Aboriginal people undertaking tertiary study at universities around Australia in the wake of MOSA's establishment; and of changing government priorities and increased funding for Aboriginal research and education that saw the number of Australian universities engaged in Aboriginal research and teaching swell to such an extent that Monash became marginal in the new environment. Finding the letter with the shocking letterhead during my final week in the University Archives was a real 'Eureka' moment; I literally whooped with relief! It was not that it contained anything of a revelatory nature – the priest merely reported on mundane matters concerning a number of MOSA students – it was more a matter of closing a circle. I still had interviews to conduct, but locating the letter helped to confirm in my mind that it was time to write.

The cornerstone of Monash's Indigenous programs, MIC in its various iterations is the main focus of this book, although MOSA, the Gippsland Centre for Koori Studies, and Yulendj are also included. Taking a roughly chronological approach and utilising the rich (though uneven) records of the Monash University Archives, its main theme is change, internal and external. Changes in name, location, personnel, and structure, affected the programs' ability to bring about positive change for Aboriginal people. Among the wide array of factors considered, the role of individuals and the role of context, or wider events, stand out as key determinants of change. From the outset, the Centre was led by people of exceptional talent, foresight and ability; passionate individuals committed to making a difference in Aboriginal peoples' lives. Strong personalities also led Monash's other Indigenous programs. Several of these leaders, notably Dr Colin Tatz, the CRAA's founder and inaugural Director, and Professor Merle Ricklefs, a key person in the establishment of MOSA, were outsiders, newcomers to Australia. Not having grown up in a society where Aboriginal peoples' second-class status was normalised, they viewed the situation with fresh eyes, asked different questions, exhibited new outrage, and sought bold new solutions to the problems they perceived in Australia. Reflecting on this, Emeritus Professor of Law, Louis Waller, called to mind a Yiddish proverb that in English translates as 'a guest for a while sees for a mile'. The outsider, he explained, is often 'equipped with a better pair of glasses than many insiders whose glasses are inevitably smeared by a variety of things, like self-interest'. However, it is also true that, having left their native land and chosen Australia, the newcomers had high hopes of their adopted country which the impoverished situation of Aboriginal people most likely upset. Viewed in this light, their efforts to redress this can be seen as an important part of their own (self-interested) self-identification as Australian. In any case, they were joined by Australian-born Indigenous and non-Indigenous men and women who refused to accept the status quo; who knew how things worked, and pressed on regardless.

Each Director brought a different set of life experiences and skills, personality and temperament to the role; each left his or her mark on Monash's Indigenous programs in different ways. Yet unpacking the puzzle of leadership is about more than determining whether

INTRODUCTION

individuals were sufficiently inspirational, motivational, and forward-thinking to make change happen; close attention must also be paid to the political, economic and social context within which they worked. Change is often easier to effect at certain times than others regardless of one's efforts. Then it's a matter of recognising that the time is ripe for change and having the courage and audacity, or 'chutzpa', as Tatz would say, to act.

This is a story of people with plenty of chutzpa. Chapter one examines Tatz's efforts to establish and maintain the CRAA during the 1960s, a time of growing political unrest and increased awakening to the plight of Aboriginal people. A political scientist and recent émigré from South Africa, Tatz's research interests informed the Centre's early research priorities and determined its focus on contemporary Aboriginal issues. The story of his successor, Dr Elizabeth Eggleston, Director from 1972 to 1976, is told in chapter two. Eggleston's background in law and passion for social justice allowed her to make significant inroads into Aboriginal communities in Victoria, expanding the Centre's work in an era of growth in Aboriginal affairs. Colin Bourke became the first Aboriginal Director in 1977. His emphasis on 'Aboriginalisation' runs through chapter three which covers the period 1977–97, taking in the Directorships of Bourke, Dr Eve Fesl and Sharon Firebrace. Covering a similar time period, 1983–97, chapter four examines the establishment and work of MOSA. Bringing the story up to the present, the recent history of Monash's Indigenous programs is told in chapter five.

As a non-Indigenous person, I benefited greatly from the advice of the Indigenous and non-Indigenous members of the Steering Committee established to oversee the writing of this book: Emeritus Professor Graeme Davison, Professor Lynette Russell, Emeritus

Professor Colin Bourke, Professor Andrew Markus, and Jason Brailey. In the end, however, the views expressed in this book are my own, not those of the Steering Committee, or the University. I was commissioned to write a critical history that everyone agreed would probably (perhaps inevitably, by virtue of its subject matter) be mostly positive. And that is what has happened.

Chapter 1

THE CENTRE, 1964–70

Colin Tatz tells the following story: 'So, you've got a South African, a Canadian and a Pom who are taking an interest in Aboriginal affairs'. The first part sounds like a joke, but the context is far from funny and there's no punch-line. South African-born Tatz was referring to fact that apart from himself and anthropologists Diane McEachern (later Barwick, born in Canada) and Jeremy Beckett (born in England), all outsiders, very few (if any) researchers were interested in the contemporary situation in Aboriginal affairs in Australia during the 1960s, a sign of the pervasiveness of the dying race theory which, even then, still held sway. A wall of 'secrecy and silence' surrounded the status of Aborigines 'incarcerated' on missions and reserves, and very little was known about how Aboriginal people lived in cities and towns. This insensitivity to the needs of Aboriginal people, and pretense 'that white administration and white laws and special laws [hadn't] impinged' on them, lit a fire that burned deep inside Tatz: 'I got very angry that this should be the state of play in what I thought was … the ultimate democratic country and the ultimate in human rights thinking, the country that boasted … the world's best practice in terms of social welfare legislation … the basic wage … rights for women and all the rest of it.' Turning his anger to good use, Tatz established the Centre for Research into Aboriginal Affairs at Monash University in 1964, thereby setting in train a series of events which saw Monash become a leader in Indigenous research, education, and employment.

Tatz's Jewish parents, like most white South Africans, had black servants. Growing up in Johannesburg in an environment where black people were 'berated, abused, demeaned and dehumanized' exposed him from a young age to the injustice of systemic racial discrimination and abuse. After studying Arts and Law at Natal University in Pietermaritzburg, he completed a Masters thesis, later published as *Shadow and Substance in South Africa: A Study in Land and Franchise Policies Affecting Africans, 1910–1960*. Offered a PhD scholarship at The Australian National University in Canberra, Tatz left South Africa with his wife and young child at the end of 1960, the rationalised complicity or collaboration in racism that life there demanded having become intolerable to him. Once in Australia 'it took him no more than two days to read the literature on contemporary Aboriginal affairs. There was absolutely nothing!' According to one of his referees for the job at Monash, Tatz had a 'wholly magnificent ability to get on with officials' that opened doors that were closed to other researchers. Granted full access to records and permits to visit Aboriginal communities in the Northern Territory, his doctoral thesis exposed the gulf that existed between policy aims and claims on the one hand, and realities on the other. When a job came up at Monash University, Tatz applied. Appointed a lecturer in the Faculty of Economics and Politics, he commenced work on 1 April 1964.

Tatz had been at Monash less than a month when he proposed the establishment of a 'Bureau of Aboriginal Affairs'. He had in mind a body like the South African Institute of Race Relations, a non-government, non-partisan, research body that produced annual reports on the current situation in South Africa. At the end of April 1964, Tatz wrote to the Vice Chancellor, J.A.L. Matheson, laying out his vision for a unit that would study the current problems that Aboriginal people were facing in society. This focus on the present made his proposal different from the newly established Australian Institute of Aboriginal Studies (AIAS) in Canberra whose mandate was to study the past. The rationale for the AIAS was 'to record language, song, art, material culture, ceremonial life and social structure before those traditions perished in the face of European ways', a further sign that Aborigines were still viewed as a dying race. Utterly appalled at the shortsightedness of this focus, Tatz argued a case for bridging the 'gaps in our knowledge of the life and conditions of Aborigines throughout Australia' today. He recognised a degree of overlap with Charles Rowley's Social Science Research Council (SSRC) funded project into matters affecting the social life and conditions of Aborigines, but saw no problem with this; to the contrary, he anticipated inheriting Rowley's sources, materials and findings at the expiration of his three-year project.

The Bureau, as Tatz conceived it, was to be a 'permanent organization' that would act as a repository of information as well as a generator of research and ideas. Importantly, he stressed that he was not seeking 'the creation of another learned, academic society'. Instead the 'participation of all interested in the Aboriginal question' – administrators, missionaries, pastoralists, activists, researchers, and Aborigines – would be sought. Tatz explained that he wanted the Bureau to assist administrators and others in developing a 'greater knowledge and understanding of the Australian Aborigines and of the relations that exist *or should exist* between them and the rest of the Australian community'. More than that, he wanted the Bureau to 'frame and advocate proposals on race relations, Aboriginal social and economic and legal conditions and education facilities'.

It was a bold and innovative proposal, especially for a young academic, but it was one that fitted with Monash's ethos of being responsive to its external environment. Matheson, although supportive, queried Tatz's statement of implied endorsement. In his proposal Tatz had written: *'It is suggested* that there is a need for [such an] organization'; Matheson wanted to know 'who suggests?' Having discussed the matter with the Directors of Native Affairs in the Northern Territory and Queensland, with mission authorities, and with academics, Tatz saw no need to dissemble: 'The suggestion', he replied, 'is primarily my own'. Exceedingly self-assured, Tatz redrafted his proposal into a submission for Monash's Professorial Board in June 1964. In this he emphasised the 'enabling' nature of the Bureau and its work: 'I see the Bureau as an "action" research body', he explained. He was careful to point out, however, that it would 'not be a "do-good" organisation', or even a 'pressure group in the ordinary sense of the term'. The Professorial Board appointed a Committee, chaired by Professor Don Cochrane, Dean of the Faculty of Economics and Politics, to report on the desirability of establishing a Bureau of Aboriginal Affairs. The Committee endorsed Tatz's proposal, but suggested that the name be changed to 'Aboriginal Research Centre'; this was later changed to 'Centre for Research into Aboriginal Affairs' (CRAA), a name that more accurately reflected the Centre's proposed activities.

Matheson approved the establishment of four Centres during his time as Vice Chancellor. The first, in early 1964, was the Centre of South East Asian Studies, proposed by Foundation Professor of History, J.D. Legge. The CRAA was the second. Formally constituted

THE CENTRE, 1964–70

Colin Tatz
Source: Colin Tatz

by a resolution of the University Council on 14 December 1964, its stated purpose was 'to undertake itself, and to stimulate elsewhere, research into such fields as Aboriginal demography, legal status, health, education, employment, vocational training, housing, and social change; and to publish the results of its research'. The Centre was also to provide 'information on matters relating to Aborigines'. A notice announcing the Centre's establishment appeared in newspapers around the country. Among the first to offer congratulations on Monash's initiative was Dr Charles Duguid, a South Australian-based campaigner for Aboriginal rights who offered to 'give whatever help I can'. Duguid was keen to share his wisdom, gained over forty years of campaigning, but what the Centre really needed was financial help. In recommending the establishment of the Centre, the Professorial Board had agreed that it 'should not call upon the University for funds other than the use of the services of Mr Tatz and some secretarial help to be provided by the Faculty of Economics and Politics'. It was up to the Centre – which meant it was up to Tatz – to 'seek assistance from outside sources for research projects'.

In the beginning, Tatz *was* the Centre, although officially only half of his time was devoted to it, the other half being taken up with lecturing duties. The Professorial Board recommended that an Advisory Board, comprising Monash and non-Monash members, be appointed to advise on the scope and functions of the Centre, and that Tatz 'should act as provisional secretary of the Centre and the Advisory Board and be charged with its general administration'. Representatives of governmental, mission and private interests concerned with Aboriginal affairs were approached to serve as members of the Advisory Board, including: Reverend Frank Engel, secretary, National Missionary Council; Professor R.H. Black, School of Public Health and Tropical Medicine, University of Sydney; Joseph McGinness, president, Federal Council for Aboriginal Advancement; George Warwick Smith, secretary, Commonwealth Department of Territories; and Charles Rowley, Director of the SSRC Aborigines Project. The first meeting of the twenty-member Board was scheduled for October 1965, some ten months after the establishment of the Centre. In the meantime the work of the Centre commenced with the Monash members of the Advisory Board acting as an executive. The Chairman of the Professorial Board Committee, Cochrane, became Chairman of the Centre's Advisory Board. Other Monash members included: Professors R.R. Andrews (Dean, Faculty of Medicine), F.R. Beasley (Faculty of Law), S.R. Davis (Politics), A.J. Marshall (Zoology), and M.G. Marwick (Anthropology and Sociology), and Drs Ian Turner (History), and Tatz.

Tatz's official title was changed from 'provisional secretary' to 'executive officer' at the first executive meeting of Centre's Advisory Board in April 1965. The meeting's minutes prompted a prickly response from Jim Butchart, Deputy Registrar, who questioned Tatz's authority to restyle himself thus, and criticised the provisional secretary (namely Tatz) for the overly discursive style of the minutes which were 'not nearly punctilious enough'. At this early stage in the life of the Centre, Butchart was anxious that the 'paperwork should not get out of gear'. He was not, however, 'anxious … to get into the act' with Tatz; rather he expected Cochrane, as chairman of the Centre's Board, to bring Tatz into line. Rebuking Butchart instead, Cochrane made it clear that Tatz's new title was 'intentional', that errors could easily be fixed, and that the style of the minutes was 'the most appropriate and … most helpful' for the members of the Centre's Board given its organisational structure. When Tatz assumed the title of 'Director' in 1967, no objections were raised.

Fifteen-year old Sue McLean (later Stevenson), a junior stenographer in the politics department, performed secretarial duties for Tatz and the Centre from 1965. The embryonic Centre's numbers grew that year when Elizabeth Eggleston joined the team. A Melbourne lawyer, Eggleston read about the Centre's establishment in the *Age*; she got in touch with Tatz who convinced her to undertake a PhD on Aboriginal people and the law. Supervised by Professor David Derham, Dean of Law, and mentored by Tatz, Eggleston was based in the Law school, but she was drawn in to CRAA activities by Tatz's relentless pursuit of justice for Aboriginal people. With Professor Louis Waller, Faculty of Law, Colin Campbell, a local barrister, and Eggleston, Tatz devised an unofficial legal aid system for Aboriginal people in Victoria that was run out of the CRAA. They mimeographed 'thousands of little pamphlets … [on] "What to do when arrested"' which they distributed among Aboriginal communities. The number of phone calls Tatz received from police across the state, sometimes in the middle of the night, and from Aboriginal people exercising their right to legal representation was, for him, proof of the scheme's success.

Other 'action research' initiatives followed. In 1965 Tatz became the Victorian Aborigines Advancement League's representative on the Victorian government's Aborigines Welfare Board. Approached for assistance in developing a research program relating to the health of Victorian Aboriginal communities, he coordinated negotiations between the Victorian Health Department, the Aborigines Welfare Board and Monash academics that resulted in the launch of a systematic study aimed at improving Aboriginal health to be run out of the Centre. The Faculty of Medicine contributed funds towards the employment of a researcher on the project, however staffing issues saw the project deferred during 1966. With assistance from the Australian Research Grants Committee (ARGC) in 1966–67, and help from researchers at the ANU, a statistical analysis of the Victorian Aboriginal population was undertaken that showed it to be more than twice as large as previously thought. In contrast to the official census conducted in 1966 which produced a figure of 1750 persons, the Centre's survey concluded that there were at least 4400 Aboriginal people in Victoria. Tatz intended to utilise this new demographic information in a revised health study, but other projects took precedence and it was not until the 1970s that health returned to the Centre's agenda.

A small grant from the SSRC Aborigines Project enabled Tatz and Professor Fred Gruen, an agricultural economist, to undertake research into Aboriginal employment on cattle stations in Northern Australia during 1965. Rowley, in authorising the grant, anticipated that the research would feed into his work, and would also result in a seminar on Aboriginal employment to be run by the Centre. The timing was propitious. In February 1965 the North Australian Workers Union lodged an application with the Commonwealth Conciliation and Arbitration Commission to vary the *Cattle Station Industry (NT) Award, 1951* to include Aboriginal pastoral workers. The Commission heard evidence in Alice Springs in the winter of 1965 and delivered its decision in March the following year, granting equal wages to Aboriginal people in the pastoral industry, but delaying their implementation until 1968.

On 23–25 May 1966, the Centre hosted a residential seminar on 'The Problems of Aboriginal Employment, Wages and Training' at Monash. Reflecting Tatz's goal of inclusivity, sixty participants were involved, only one-third of whom were academics with the remainder representing other interests: state and federal Aboriginal departments (fourteen people); mining, pastoral, missionary and parliamentary interests (thirteen people); trade unions (three people); and Aboriginal welfare and advancement groups (ten people, including six Aboriginal and Torres Strait Islanders). Writing to congratulate the Vice Chancellor on his sponsorship of the seminar, Diane Barwick observed that it was 'the first occasion on which government officials, academics and representatives of unions, church missions and welfare organisations [had] been brought together to exchange views'. An anthropologist at the ANU, Barwick felt that 'the opportunity to meet and discuss informally' was as important as the 'new information provided in the papers and general discussion'. The highlight for Tatz was watching Aboriginal leaders – Jacob Abednego, Joe McGinness, Kath Walker, Charles Perkins, Bert Groves and John Moriarty – talk with people 'whom they had hitherto known [only] as names on paper'. The outcome was the creation of 'a bridge of communication between parties' who typically ignored or 'publicly [condemned] the action or point of view of the other'. Secretary of the Federal Council for the Advancement of Aboriginal and Torres Strait Islanders, Stan Davey felt that only a university could have achieved such an outcome, for had any other interest group attempted such a feat it would have failed: 'Emotions run high and suspicion is a constant barrier'. Echoing Davey, Ian Spalding, editor of the journal *On Aboriginal Affairs*, felt that the seminar demonstrated the extent to which universities could contribute 'to research and policy leadership in this important but neglected area'.

The Wages and Employment seminar put the CRAA on the map, raising its public and official profile. Amid growing concerns about the Centre's capacity to sustain its workload, Tatz began making plans for a second seminar. The Centre's Advisory Board encouraged him to finish his current projects before incurring any further commitments, but that was not how Tatz operated. An equally successful seminar on 'Aboriginal Education' was held in 1967. Both seminars resulted in publications that further boosted the Centre's profile and remained standards in the literature for years to come: *Aborigines in the Economy: Employment, Wages and Training* (edited by Ian Sharp and Tatz), and *Aborigines and Education* (edited by Sydney Dunn and Tatz).

THE CENTRE, 1964–70

During the Centre's first year of operation, Tatz had approached several large philanthropic bodies for financial support, but without success. In the wake of the Wages and Employment and Education seminars, he approached the Bernard van Leer Foundation, a charitable organisation based in the Netherlands, for funding for a project on Aboriginal pre-schools in Victoria. Established with broad humanitarian goals in the aftermath of World War Two, the Bernard van Leer Foundation had shifted its focus to young children and education in the mid 1960s, and had funded its first international project (in Jamaica) in 1966. Tatz, in his capacity as a member of the Victorian Aborigines Welfare Board, knew that the Foundation was looking for projects to fund.

Detailing the need for Aboriginal pre-schools, Tatz argued that preschool training would increase Aboriginal 'children's powers of self-expression and enrich their social experience' leading to 'better school performance and increased social adaptability'. More than that, he claimed that effective preschool training could act as a vehicle for 'reconciliation between Aboriginal and European values', providing Aboriginal children 'with functional, learned responses to cope with the crisis of cultural identification' which occurred frequently at adolescence. Tatz imagined preschools where Aboriginal children would have 'alongside their standard picture books, pictures and books of famous men and great legends of their own people, tribal and acculturated'. The time was ripe for action. The Victorian government, having previously had no specific policy on Aboriginal preschools, had committed funds to the building of three preschools in Aboriginal communities at Lake Tyers, Rumalara Settlement and Swan Hill. The Centre for Research into Aboriginal Affairs wished to play an active role in the devising of programs and evaluation of needs and results at these facilities, Tatz explained, for 'should a carefully planned and evaluated project show tangible results, an important breakthrough in Aboriginal education will have been achieved'.

On the grounds that such an evaluation would need to take place over three years, and would attract personnel, equipment and travel costs, Tatz requested a grant of $44,650. His request was approved. A six-month investigatory period – during which the parameters of the three-year program would be defined, and for which additional funding was provided (bringing the total grant up to $50,000) – was set up in the first instance. Subsequently, Tatz and his research assistant, Lorna Lippman visited New Zealand where Lex Grey of the Maori Education Fellowship had established play-centres in which Maori mothers were the teachers. This was the model Tatz wished to employ in Victoria, but other forces prevailed, resulting in the establishment of more traditional kindergartens.

In 1967 the Centre – which by then comprised Tatz, Lippman, McLean, and Eggleston – moved from the Faculty of Economics and Politics to the Department of Anthropology and Sociology. The year 1967 was a big one in Aboriginal affairs, and a critical one for the Centre. In May a referendum was held which cleared the way for the Commonwealth to make special laws in relation to Aboriginal people. One outcome of the referendum was the establishment of the Council for Aboriginal Affairs (CAA), an advisory body comprising Dr H.C. 'Nugget' Coombs, former governor of the Reserve Bank; Professor W.E.H Stanner, a respected anthropologist; and Barrie Dexter, a senior public servant and former diplomat. The Council, which operated out of the newly established Office of Aboriginal Affairs (OAA) located within the Prime Minister's Department, was intended to provide government with expert advice on Aboriginal affairs. A request from Matheson for financial assistance for the Centre was sitting on Coombs desk when he took up his position as Chair of the CAA. The Vice Chancellor's request was denied. This coupled with the University's experience in connection with financing the Centre's two residential seminars (it had contributed nearly $5000 from recurrent funds), led Matheson to conclude that Monash 'must either finance [the] Centre ... or abandon it'. Despite the magnitude of the van Leer grant, its funds were tied to research associated with the preschool project and could not be used to finance the Centre. Since there was no longer any point in 'pretending' that it could be conducted without cost to the University, Matheson declared that the time had come to consider 'the future of the Centre'.

The Centre's Future

As a first step, it was decided to change the composition of the Centre's Advisory Board so as to include only members of staff at Monash University thereby reducing the costs associated with bringing people to Melbourne for Board meetings. This also brought the Centre more into line with other Centres at Monash, and made the Board less 'unwieldy'. Further, 'in view of the financial situation' and the likely absence of Tatz who was due to go on study leave, it was decided that no seminar would be conducted in 1968. Tatz spent the first few months of 1968 in New Zealand, and the latter half on sabbatical in Canada. Before leaving for Canada, he met with Coombs and Dexter, both of whom 'indicated considerable interest in the Centre's work and future', according to Tatz. 'They expressed a desire to see the Centre remain viable', he explained to Matheson, but were constrained in their ability to help for 'fear of other universities making similar requests'. Tatz's priority was to secure funding sufficient to cover Lippman's salary, a task he achieved by convincing Coombs and Dexter to commission the Centre to do a piece of contract research.

The Centre's future was still uncertain in 1969. Concerned to clarify the University's position, Matheson asked the Centre's Board to prepare answers to the following questions:

1. Should the Centre continue and, if so, in what form?
2. Has the work so far performed by the Centre fulfilled the original objects or does experience suggest that the aim of the Centre should be now changed?
3. What staff and budget will be required for the Centre to function in the preferred manner?
4. What should be the relationship between the Centre and the Department of Anthropology and Sociology?
5. Is it possible for the Director to be a full-time member of the Department staff, devoting to the Centre the time that he would normally have available for personal research?

In private communication with the new Chairman of the Centre's Board, Professor M.G. Swift, Matheson made it clear that he was most anxious 'to make sure that the Centre really is doing a sound job which really justifies any budget that the Board of the Centre may recommend'.

At a special meeting of the Centre's Board in September 1969 it was agreed that there were 'grounds for continuing the Centre'; that the staffing of the Centre should be half of Tatz's time, a full-time clerical assistant and a research assistant; that Tatz and the clerical assistant should be financed from University central funds, and that additional university funds be supplied to meet stationary, travel and accommodation expenses; and that financial assistance be sought from the OAA to meet the costs of a research assistant and national seminar program. However, this view was not put to the Professorial Board, and so was not relayed via official channels to Matheson, because of uncertainty over Tatz's position. Tatz was offered a Chair in Politics at the University of Waikato (New Zealand) at the end of 1969, but turned it down in favour of a position at the University of New England (Armidale, New South Wales) which, by February 1970, looked unlikely to eventuate: 'Happily I'm not going anywhere', Tatz trumpeted.

While awaiting the Board's official response on the matter of the Centre's future, Matheson was approached by the National ABSCHOL Director, Ian Langman, who complimented Monash's leadership in the study of Aboriginal Affairs. A committee of the National Union of Australian University Students, ABSCHOL was set up during the 1960s to support university scholarships for Aboriginal students. The federal government introduced the Aboriginal Study Grants Scheme (ABSTUDY) for Aboriginal students in tertiary studies from the beginning of the academic year in 1969. However, when it became apparent that the lack of applications for both schemes was due to the lack of suitably qualified Aboriginal students, ABSCHOL began encouraging Aboriginal tertiary education in other ways, such as by 'calling on all universities to set up centres for study into Aboriginal Affairs'. Unaware of the Centre's precarious state, Langman implored Matheson to urge his colleagues on the Australian Vice-Chancellor's Committee to establish units like the CRAA 'in their own universities'.

In early 1970, in a widely publicised address to the Sydney University Liberal Club, the federal Minister in charge of Aboriginal Affairs, W.C. (Bill) Wentworth criticised Australian universities for their lack of interest in Aboriginal studies and problems. Calling on universities to devote more of their energies 'towards the academic side of the problem', Wentworth declared: 'Academic study is not divorced from welfare. It has a practical value.' Tatz could not have agreed more. He drew Matheson's attention to press reports of Wentworth's speech and announced that, after months of negotiation, the OAA had finally 'crystallized its policy towards the Centre', selecting it 'as an appropriate body' to undertake research of interest to government. The OAA wanted the Centre's (or more accurately Tatz's) assistance in developing a comprehensive Aboriginal Studies program. Tatz saw this as a clear sign that the Centre should continue and was 'thrilled' that his hard work had paid off. He expected Matheson to feel the same, but the Vice Chancellor's reaction was cool. Matheson wanted to know the Board's official position on the Centre's long-term future before any decisions regarding new projects were made.

The Centre's Board met in March 1970. Tempering Tatz's enthusiasm, the Board expressed a 'cautious willingness to proceed'. The research conducted by members of the Centre, the service provided to outside bodies, and the role the Centre had played in 'seeking solutions to problems of social relevance which might not [otherwise] receive proper attention if judged solely by their academic significance' were all presented as reasons for continuing the Centre. However, Chairman of the Board, Swift, wanted the Centre to play a more 'central part within Monash'; this was in response to an observation, expressed by Matheson, that most of the research on Aboriginal issues undertaken by staff at Monash was 'conducted independently of the Centre'. Although Tatz took exception to this statement (which he read, somewhat dramatically, as signaling the end of the Centre), a major program of inter-disciplinary seminars involving staff with 'an active or specialised interest in some aspect of Aboriginal life' from across the university was added to the Centre's list of activities for the forthcoming year.

More troubling was the question of the Centre's financial viability. Stevenson recalled that Tatz 'spent an inordinate amount of time in the early years trying to get funds to keep the Centre going'. This is reflected in the records of the Centre's Board. Swift openly acknowledged that the question of funding had been 'problematic' since the Centre's inception. Although inaugurated on the premise that central funding from the University would not be sought, this premise had never been maintained. With insufficient funds coming from outside sources, host departments – first Economics and Politics, later Anthropology and Sociology – had provided support for administrative expenses. The Board resolved therefore to ask the OAA for an annual grant of $1000 to cover administrative expenses. Should this request be denied, the Board suggested a more equitable sharing of the burden across the university, reasoning that 'because of its inter-disciplinary nature, all faculties concerned should be asked to contribute at least small sums annually' for the maintenance of the Centre. Regardless, the Board felt that the Centre's work was of 'sufficient importance' to merit ongoing University support, 'especially in the light of the relatively small sum needed'. It was estimated that $11,175 was required to keep the Centre alive, being the annual cost of one-half of a Director's salary, and the salaries of a full-time clerical assistant and full-time research assistant. Previously the cost of a research assistant had not formed part of the universities financial burden, being paid for by grants from the OAA. However, in light of the potential new opportunities accruing in connection with the OAA, asking more of the university probably seemed only fair.

The burgeoning relationship between the Centre and the Office of Aboriginal Affairs was given as a further reason to continue the Centre. More circumspect than Tatz, Swift noted in his report that it *'would seem* that a sound relationship has been established' with the OAA. Swift was right to be cautious, as much of this relationship was built on potential promises and tentative undertakings between Tatz and Dexter, now Director of the OAA. Tatz's trusting nature, optimism, and faith in the Centre's future blinded him to the weakness of linking the Centre's future so firmly to the OAA. Other Board members, including Swift, were swayed by his confidence and by their own desire to believe in a positive outcome, Swift reporting that the Centre's Board 'welcomed two new projects, both of which *may be* wholly financed by the Office': the Aboriginal Studies Syllabus project flagged earlier by Tatz, and a History Project on white-Aboriginal relations in the Riverina area. While plans were also mooted for a third national seminar, this time on Aboriginal Health (for which financial assistance from the OAA would also be sought), much hope hung on the two new projects, especially the Aboriginal Studies Syllabus Project which was forecast to bring more than $20,000 to Monash.

On 19 May 1970, Dexter wrote to Tatz asking whether the OAA could be represented on the Centre's Board. The wording of his request was significant: 'I have been wondering, whether, in view of our increasing contact with *your* Centre, there would be any advantage in my Office being represented on the Centre's Board.' The extent to which Dexter identified Tatz with the Centre was telling, and would prove important in the days and weeks to come.

Although Dexter made it clear that the OAA's 'continued interest in and support of the Centre in no way' depended on this arrangement, it was not an offer Tatz or the University could refuse. A second letter from Dexter arrived that day, bearing the news that Wentworth had approved a grant to cover the Centre's administrative expenses to June 1971. This was good news indeed, for the Committee of Deans had rejected the idea of cross-faculty financial support.

Within days of these communications, Tatz had been offered the foundation Chair of Politics at the University of New England and had decided, regretfully, to leave Monash. It was not an easy decision to make. Tatz felt a 'moral obligation' to the CRAA, but believed that 'it had been taken as far as it could go within the framework of the existing university policy and budgeting ability'. After informing the Vice Chancellor of his decision, Tatz's job was to tell Dexter. Matheson wanted Tatz to convey a clear message that while Monash would 'try and keep the Centre going at a modest level ... budgetary pressure would prevent our doing anything more unless outside funding could be found'. Putting it more bluntly, Matheson remarked that 'if the Commonwealth wanted to keep [the Centre] going it had better make a regular grant for the Director's salary'. This was a new development, brought about, in all likelihood, by Tatz's disclosure that the proposed grant from the OAA for the Aboriginal Syllabus project had been seen by the OAA as a 'grant to Tatz: it was not a Centre project'. It had been represented as a Centre project, Tatz explained, 'because the Office could not make grants to individuals' and so had 'intended to offer the funds to Monash for distribution to the individual researcher'. However, as a consequence of Tatz's move to Armidale, it was 'probable that this grant [would] now be offered to New England'.

Tatz met with Dexter at the end of May. His subsequent report to Matheson was uncharacteristically brief. Dexter, Tatz reported, 'felt strongly that the Centre should continue'. On the question of the OAA contributing to the salary of a new director, Tatz quoted Dexter as saying '"that doesn't frighten me in the least"'. Such hearsay assertions of support were no longer enough. Matheson wanted 'a clear understanding ... with the [OAA] on what financial allocations could be relied on'; he wanted proof of support, and he wanted it to come from a source other than Tatz. Matheson asked the new chairman of the Centre's Board, Professor Basil Hetzel to invite Dexter for 'a private discussion ... in order to discover his confidential view on the future of the Centre'. In the meantime, given Tatz's assurance that he 'had no intention of starting another Centre' at New England, the Centre's Board resolved that, to be effective, the Centre needed a full-time Director and an upgraded secretary, as well as appropriate funds for research and other activities. Hetzel secured the Vice Chancellor's agreement to provide half the estimated budget of $15,000 on the condition that the other half was provided by the OAA.

Dexter endorsed this plan, but final approval rested with the Minister. When, in November 1970, Wentworth had still not signed off on the agreement, and Dexter reported that 'communication with his Minister [was] well nigh impossible', Tatz, ever the pragmatist, suggested a new plan. If the worst came to the worst, the Centre, he claimed, could make do – 'albeit in a crippled way' – on the University's contribution alone, an annual budget of $7500 being just enough to cover the cost of a secretary and half of a new Director's salary. Tatz, who was due to leave Monash in less than a month's time, presented this as a matter of urgency to the Budget Office, the Committee of Deans and the Vice Chancellor. He was adamant that his successor needed to be named, and funds made available if the Centre was to continue. Uncomfortable with the feeling of being 'rushed', the University deferred its decision while awaiting the Minister's response.

A telegram from Dexter arrived at the beginning of December: 'MINISTER IN CHARGE HAS DECIDED NOT REPEAT NOT TO CONTRIBUTE TO CENTRE'S COSTS'. Matheson found the Minister's decision 'both surprising and ... very disappointing'. With Tatz gone, and the hoped for funds unforthcoming, his immediate reaction was to close the Centre. Informed that plans were already in train for a conference on Aboriginal Health to be held in 1972, he reversed his decision, but allocated a mere $5000 towards the running of the Centre in 1971 and 1972, being just enough to allow the Centre to continue its operation on a 'minimum scale'. The most important reason for the Minister's refusal to endorse the proposed grant, Matheson later learned, was his 'reluctance to assume responsibility of an indefinite duration'. Rather than continue to rely on grants from the government, Dexter advised the Vice Chancellor that it was 'really for Monash University itself to decide whether it wishes to continue the Centre'. If the Centre was to continue past 1972, and this was by no means certain, Matheson was adamant that the 'old boy methods' employed by Tatz would have to be replaced 'by more formal communications'. Things were about to change.

Chapter 2

EMBEDDING AND EXPANDING, 1971–76

The 1970s witnessed profound changes in the administration and politicisation of Aboriginal affairs. Shifts in thinking occurred as new paradigms emerged to replace previous policies and practices of assimilation. New Aboriginal leaders, many adopting the rhetoric of the US Black Power movement, embraced new forms of protest, new goals and new ideals, symbolised in the raising of tents at Parliament House in Canberra in 1972 in protest over Land Rights. Old political alliances were questioned as Aboriginal activists sought 'black control of black affairs'. The impact of these changes on Monash's Centre for Research into Aboriginal Affairs during the first half of the decade was felt mainly in the growing emphasis the new Director, Dr Elizabeth Eggleston, placed on consulting and involving Aboriginal people in the work of the Centre. Eggleston was Director of the CRAA for just five years (ten months of which were spent in North America on study leave). What she managed to achieve during that time was nothing short of remarkable. She inherited a Centre on the brink of being closed, an 'emergency operation' functioning on a minimum budget with minimum staff; within four years she was Director of a Centre with a surplus that was being spent on employing Aboriginal research assistants. Plans were in place for the appointment of a full-time Director when news of her terrible illness broke in January 1976; she died of cancer three months later.

The daughter of future Monash Chancellor Sir Richard Eggleston, Elizabeth Eggleston was appointed Director of the CRAA on a half-time basis in April 1971, and was promoted to Senior Lecturer in the Faculty of Law, also on a half-time basis, at the same time. Lorna Lippman's services were retained as research officer and Sue McLean, now Stevenson, continued as secretary. As Director, Eggleston's duties included: the administration of the Centre; the stimulation of research into Aboriginal Affairs at Monash; the general coordination of Aboriginal Affairs research in various departments and faculties; the conduct of both national and internal seminars and workshops; general supervision of postgraduate students; and the conduct of her own personal research. Eggleston, newly minted PhD in hand, was relatively inexperienced in academic administration, but her credentials were otherwise excellent. A graduate of the University of Melbourne (BA, LLB Hons) and Berkeley (LLM), Eggleston's interest in Aboriginal affairs was sparked following a visit to a Native American reservation. It made a deep and lasting impression on her, not least because it made her aware of how little she knew about Australia's Aboriginal people. On her return to Australia, Eggleston worked as a solicitor in Melbourne for three years before commencing a PhD on Aborigines and the law at Monash where she was supervised by Professor David Derham, Dean of Law, and Professor Louis Waller, and mentored by Dr Colin Tatz. The infant Law School's first doctoral scholar, she was appointed a lecturer in the Faculty of Law at Monash at the end of 1969. When she became Director of the CRAA, it moved to the Law School with her.

Elizabeth Eggleston
Source: Monash Archives

Eggleston brought to the job of Director a different skill set, personality and temperament to Tatz. Where Tatz was confident and outspoken, Eggleston was quiet and unassuming. Secretary to both Directors, Stevenson described Eggleston as 'solid [and] ... very calm'; she never got 'excited about anything, or angry about anything'. Several of Eggleston's referees for the position of Director commented on her tendency to 'underrate her own abilities' and 'undervalue her own work'. Derham regarded her 'diffidence about her own talents' as a limitation that resulted in her being 'more retiring' than she needed to be, yet this proved advantageous in her relationships with Aboriginal people. Unthreatening, Eggleston was able to move easily among Aboriginal communities who profited from her experience in a wide range of legal matters. During the course of her PhD candidature, she spent time among Aboriginal communities in Victoria, South Australia and Western Australia, studying the actual workings of the law in places where Aborigines lived. She took the 'time and trouble', Waller recalled, 'to seek representation for Aborigines charged with offences, to find witnesses, to listen to their stories'. 'Tireless, conscientious and meticulous', Eggleston was absolutely devoted to her work. While these qualities stood her in good stead for the job ahead, it was her experience working with Tatz which most recommended her for the position of Director. Apart from Tatz himself, Eggleston was the 'person best acquainted with the Centre's work'. Further, as the recipient of a large ARGC grant, she brought both funds and status to the position.

Eggleston's first task as Director was not a pleasant one. At the request of the Vice Chancellor, she was asked to question Tatz about the 'whereabouts of books and other material formerly located in the Centre'. The inference that Tatz had taken books belonging to the Centre was quickly overturned; Tatz had only removed books that were his personal possessions. However, in doing so he had effectively removed the Centre's library, Eggleston reported, since his collection had 'formerly constituted the Centre library'. With 'no budgeting provision ... ever made for buying books', Tatz had lent his books to students privately, and Eggleston planned to continue the same practice, taking out subscriptions (at her own expense) to periodicals of local Aboriginal groups and using her own books as the basis of a renewed Centre library. The fact remained, however, that the

Centre did not have a library. More precisely, Eggleston insisted that 'a few books, a collection of press cuttings, pamphlets and whatever else can be obtained free does not constitute an *adequate library*'. Eggleston was adamant that the Centre needed a library; pushing for one became a feature of her Directorship that, sadly, was achieved as a memorial to her after her untimely death.

Eggleston began her efficient administration by implementing the recommendations for an internal seminar series made towards the end of Tatz's reign. A program of nine interdisciplinary seminars was arranged in 1971. In 1972, the papers presented the previous year were compiled into a booklet that was duplicated for sale around the University; 500 copies were made and sold for $1 each. During 1973, the monthly seminars attracted attendees of up to 120 persons, 'indicating a widespread interest in Aboriginal and racial affairs'. The list of speakers and topics that year included: Charles Rowley, 'Aborigines Enter Politics: Aboriginal Organisations and non-Aboriginal Resistance'; Bruce McGuiness, 'Urban Aborigines: The Identity Crisis'; Barry Dexter, 'The Role of an Aboriginal Agency'; and Frank Stevens, speaking on 'The Future of Aboriginal Labour in North Australia'. Eggleston herself presented a paper on 'American Indians Confront the Law'. The following year, at Eggleston's invitation, guest presenters from North America provided first-hand insights from Native America and Inuit communities. Further expanding the Centre's profile, Eggleston lectured on Aboriginal affairs to students across the University, and participated in forums conducted by ABSCOL. With Lippman, she also gave presentations to Aboriginal organisations and other non-university bodies.

EMBEDDING AND EXPANDING, 1971-76

The Centre's relationship with the Commonwealth Government had soured somewhat in the wake of the funding debacle in 1970. While not forsaking the Commonwealth Government, new avenues of funding and bases of support were sought. In her first few months as Director, Eggleston initiated a meeting with the Victorian Minister for Aboriginal Affairs, E.R. Meagher. Attended by the Vice Chancellor, the Chairman of the Centre's Board, Professor Basil Hetzel, and Eggleston, the meeting was convened for the purpose of acquainting Meagher with the Centre's activities. Whereas Tatz had served on the Victorian Aborigines Welfare Board and had thereby maintained formal connections with the goings-on of Aboriginal affairs at a local level, the Board was disbanded in 1968, which meant that new connections had to be made, and new avenues for working together explored. One way Eggleston did this was by visiting Aboriginal people in prison. A member of the Victorian Aborigines Advancement League (VAAL), Eggleston, together with other League members, was involved in the running of discussion groups for Aboriginal prisoners at Pentridge.

The unofficial legal aid service for Aboriginal people that Eggleston, Tatz, Professor Louis Waller and Colin Campbell had set up in 1965 became more formalised and moved away from the CRAA (see Chapter 1). In 1971, law students at Monash University and the University of Melbourne established a legal referral service for Aborigines that was run through the VAAL with Eggleston acting as an advisor to the students. The following year, while teaching a legal aid seminar that highlighted the needs of Aboriginal people, she co-founded (with Stewart Murray, Merle Jackomos, Geraldine Briggs, Louis Waller and others) the Victorian Aboriginal Legal Service. These and other similar activities demonstrated the Centre's unique ability to provide an 'academic contribution to the urgent needs of the Aboriginal people', and helped to win the confidence of the Victorian Aboriginal community.

Meanwhile, plans for the forthcoming national seminar on Aboriginal Health Services continued apace. Sponsorship was obtained from the Victorian Department of Aboriginal Affairs, the Secondary Schools Aboriginal Fund and Myer. The Commonwealth government also provided funds, but only after agreement about the contents of the seminar was reached. Health was Hetzel's area of expertise. The Foundation Professor of Social and Preventative Medicine at Monash, Hetzel envisioned the seminar as an exercise in 'social engineering, involving people other than health professionals, who nonetheless are very much involved in improved delivery of health care and preventative care to the Aboriginal people'.

Held over three days in May 1972, the CRAA's Aboriginal Health Services seminar was opened by the Commonwealth Minister, Peter Howson. Like previous seminars, speakers included officers of government departments, church missions, academics, medical practitioners, social workers, and others. Twenty Aboriginal people participated in the event. The seminar made a series of strongly worded recommendations, beginning with a statement about the importance of racial pride: 'in any programme of health care the integrity of Aboriginal people is crucial, therefore every attempt must be made to foster a sense of solidarity and dignity so that Aboriginal identity can be preserved and promoted.' Followed by a statement about Aboriginal involvement in Aboriginal health services – 'health programmes [must] be planned in consultation with the Aboriginal communities they are designed to serve … and carried out through the people themselves and their community leaders' – the influence of Aboriginal participants at the seminar was clear. Before 'self-determination' became the catch-cry of Aboriginal affairs, the recommendations of the CRAA's Aboriginal Health Services seminar show the desire of Aboriginal people to be self-managing. Interestingly (and importantly given how little scholarly historical research had been conducted at this point) the third recommendation revealed a nascent yet clear understanding of the historical, political and structural underpinnings of racism and its effects on Aboriginal health:

> 3. The current disastrous health situation is a by-product of the complexity and diversity of an Aboriginal society under pressure of European society. It is a total community problem and not primarily one of individual health. A strategy to meet this problem requires a comprehensive approach including a drastic improvement in education, housing and economic opportunity as well as health services.

The Aboriginal Health Services seminar underpinned changes in Aboriginal Health policy in Canberra in 1973, and resulted in the publication, *Better Health for Aborigines*.

The success of the Aboriginal Health Services seminar, like the seminars on Wages and Employment (1966), and Education (1967) before it, reinforced the CRAA's role as an 'action research' body, raised its public profile, and helped to validate and strengthen Monash's continued support for the Centre. In the wake of the seminar, the University agreed to provide just over half of the estimated $20,000 annual budget the Centre needed to continue its operations. A request for a modest grant of $1800 to cover the cost of administrative expenses was lodged with the Commonwealth Office of Aboriginal Affairs (OAA). Although similar sums had been provided in the past, the request was denied. Informing the Centre's acting chairman, Professor Scott, of this decision, Barrie Dexter, Director of the OAA, explained that such grants would not be continued, and restated his advice that it was 'really for Monash University itself to decide whether it wished to continue the Centre, and if so to make appropriate financial provision for it'. What the Centre needed to do, Dexter firmly asserted, was 'live within the annual budget provided by the University'.

The impact of Dexter's strongly worded communication was lessened somewhat by the change of government that occurred within weeks of its receipt. After twenty-three years of conservative rule, the arrival of a Labor government signaled the hope of change and reform. Even Monash's Committee of Deans smelled change in the air, remaining calm when noting the appreciable shortfall in the Centre's funds due to the Commonwealth's retraction of funding, for 'it was thought that the recent change of government might result in a review of this decision'. The Whitlam government established several new departments soon after taking office, one of which was the Department of Aboriginal Affairs. The new Minister for Aboriginal Affairs, Gordon Bryant, was well known for taking a sympathetic interest in Aboriginal issues. Prior to becoming Minister, he had been an office bearer in the VAAL and the Federal Council for Aboriginal Advancement. He was aware of the Centre's work and keen to provide assistance. Within months of taking office Bryant approved a grant of $4000 per annum for three years to 'enable the work of the Centre to proceed with a capacity for long-term planning of projects', and indicated that he was prepared to consider providing further assistance for 'special projects' as well. As part of the deal, Lippman was seconded as a consultant to the Minister.

Bryant's largesse was met with excitement and activity; immediately plans began being drawn up for the expansion of the Centre's work. Three new activities were proposed: 'Black Australian Studies' – a course for credit for undergraduates; 'Studies in Aboriginal Culture' – a course to be offered through the Centre for Continuing Education at Monash; and the development of an 'Aboriginal Resources Centre'. Inspired by the Minister's enthusiasm, Eggleston's larger vision was to use these three new initiatives, together with the CRAA's existing program of research and internal and residential seminars, as the 'foundation for the development of the Centre into the first "Race Relations Centre" in Australia'.

Expansion Plans

Outlining the 'felt need' for an undergraduate course in Black Australian Studies, Eggleston pointed to the high attendance rate at the CRAA's monthly seminars and the desire for such a course expressed by Aboriginal groups and individuals. Many Aboriginal people, she claimed, had 'been pressing for the inclusion of Black Australian Studies in one, at least, of the Australian universities as an indication of their cultural distinction from the major society and the contribution which they have made and are making to it'. Given Monash's role in establishing the CRAA, it seemed 'fitting' that it 'should be the first Australian university to present such a course'. Unbeknown to Eggleston, Dr John Hirst at La Trobe University in Melbourne's west commenced teaching Australian Aboriginal History in 1973 in response to current events.

Courses in Aboriginal Studies had also been run at Teachers' Colleges in Adelaide (1968), Bendigo (1973), and Armidale. Eggleston was aware of the course at Armidale. Run in 1971 and 1972, it had been initiated by Tatz. One of the main criticisms of the Armidale course was that 'insufficient lectures had been given by Aborigines'; out of thirteen lectures, only four had been delivered by Aboriginal people. Building on this, Eggleston proposed to 'use Aboriginal lecturers ... wherever possible' in her course. She also wanted 'special consideration ... given to Aborigines wishing to enroll, even where they are not matriculants, to encourage as many as possible to take part'. The remainder of the cohort would be drawn from undergraduates.

The syllabus Eggleston proposed in September 1973 drew on all the extant and emerging research available and reflected contemporary issues of importance to Aboriginal people:

1. The nature and function of prejudice
2. The traditional Aboriginal society
3. Historical perspectives in Aboriginal-white relations
4. Aboriginal identity
5. Present-day situation of Aborigines
6. Black self-determination
7. Land Rights
8. Contemporary Culture
9. Overseas indigenous groups

The Centre's Board expressed concerns about practical matters such as who was going to fund and run the course: questions were asked about the length of the course (one or two semesters?), and whether a quota would need to be imposed on the number of students enrolled. The Department of Anthropology and Sociology, although in favour of the introduction of such a course, made it clear that it was unable to provide any practical help. Dubious that any course for credit could be introduced before the 1975 academic year, the Centre's Board suggested that the course be offered as a pilot not-for-credit course run by the CRAA. If it 'could be demonstrated that demand for the course existed among the student body', and if sufficient outside funding could be found, a stronger case could be made for approving it for credit. The Commonwealth Department of Aboriginal Affairs agreed to sponsor the course, providing an additional grant of $3000 to assist with its establishment.

Commencing in June 1974, Black Australian Studies attracted an enrolment of fifty students, a mixture of undergraduates and members of the community. Reviewed by Monash's Higher Education Research Unit at the conclusion of the semester, the course was found to have been 'successful in achieving its stated aims'. Typical of students' replies to the question 'What do you consider the main effect the course had on you?' were: 'have learned to some extent what it means to be Aboriginal'; 'deeper insight into the authentic aims and feelings of blacks'. One student, who found the course 'invaluable', felt that she had 'begun a journey towards a better understanding of Aborigines and Europeans'. Given that Lippman, in *Words or Blows: Racial Attitudes in Australia*, published in 1973, found that some 40 percent of Victorians interviewed had attitudes towards Aborigines which varied from unfavourble to very unfavourable, the course's potential to produce 'more enlightened and sensitive' attitudes was highlighted in subsequent arguments for accreditation. Black Australian Studies was offered as a not-for-credit unit again in 1975, this time attracting an enrolment of thirty students. The smaller number of enrolments may have been a reflection of the timing of the offering, Tuesdays at 7.30pm; it may also have signaled a desire on the part of the student body for a credit-based option (which did not become available until 1979).

Eggleston's plans for expansion included two substantive course offerings – Black Australian Studies and Studies in Aboriginal Culture. The motivation for the latter course arose, she explained, 'primarily from a need expressed by part-Aboriginal people to learn more about their culture'. Many young Aboriginal people, having grown up in cities and towns, knew little of their peoples' history and culture. In some cases their relationship to Aboriginal communities and culture had been diminished, or even severed, through having been removed from their parents as children, or through moving away from their people's country. A new generation of Aboriginal leaders such as Bruce McGuiness, a student at Monash, and Bob Maza were 'intent on forging an Aboriginal consciousness grounded in Aboriginal tradition'. Responding to this need, Eggleston proposed to mount 'a continuing education course which, as distinct from the undergraduate course, would deal specifically with traditional [Aboriginal] culture'. However, given the reservations of several CRAA Board members who felt that 'tribal Aborigines might hold the view that the proper way to learn of tribal culture was to live [it]', as a first step it was decided to hold a seminar for local Aboriginal people in order to determine the purpose and nature of the course. Although originally conceived as a five-day fully funded event, in the end a more modest one-day 'Seminar on Studies in Aboriginal Culture' was held at Monash in February 1974. Rather than opt for a course on Aboriginal culture, participants agreed to form a Victorian Council for Aboriginal Culture 'away from the University at another location which would permit easy access by Aboriginal people'. The Council, responsible for organising some of the earliest Aboriginal art exhibitions in the state, affirmed and strengthened Aboriginal culture for the benefit of Aboriginal and non-Aboriginal people alike. Thus, although Eggleston's proposal did not result in a course on Aboriginal culture, it nevertheless had a positive outcome.

The third element in Eggleston's expanded vision for the CRAA was the establishment of an Aboriginal Resource Centre. The idea came directly from the Minister for Aboriginal Affairs, Bryant, who 'thought it desirable to establish [Aboriginal Resource] Centres ... in each of the state capitals, to act as focal points which could provide material and information on Aborigines and race relations for primary and secondary schools and for the public at large'. Bryant invited the CRAA to make a submission for the establishment of such a facility at Monash. With the Board's approval, Eggleston drew up a comprehensive proposal in March 1974. Building on the Centre's existing (though under-resourced) propensity to field requests for information and source material on Aborigines from students and teachers, her enlarged vision included the provision of printed and audio-visual materials to schools and the general public, and the facilitation of a panel of Aboriginal speakers who would be available on a fee-paying basis. She also proposed to staff the Resource Centre with Aboriginal employees.

When, towards the end of 1974, the Centre's Board learned that the Aboriginal Cooperative in Fitzroy (inner city Melbourne) would probably become a Resource Centre 'for Aboriginal users by virtue of its location', it reaffirmed the need for a Resource Centre at Monash whose users would 'be mainly secondary students and teachers'. The Regional Director of the Department of Aboriginal Affairs, P.F. Renkin, was invited to attend a CRAA Board meeting to discuss the matter in April 1975, a year after the original proposal had been submitted. Renkin, although supportive of the general arguments, was otherwise non-committal. Other bodies, including government agencies, were becoming involved in the provision of similar services. In light of this, the CRAA's Board felt that the success of the proposal 'was basically a matter of whether its ... activities were distinct from those performed by existing Victorian organizations'. Eggleston disagreed. For her it was a matter of having the service already supplied by the CRAA properly supported. She drew up a revised proposal in August 1975 emphasising the 'considerable ... existing demand' but the timing was against her. Scandal racked the Whitlam government and a budgetary crisis loomed. At the next CRAA Board meeting, it was noted simply that 'owing to budgetary restraints', the proposal to establish an Aboriginal Resource Centre 'would not receive financial support from the Department of Aboriginal Affairs'.

The Aboriginal Resource Centre idea was shelved, but not before it, together with the Center's proposed new course offerings, was presented as the means of developing the CRAA into a Race Relations Centre. It was a bold vision, the aim of which, Eggleston explained, 'would be to provide a better community climate of understanding towards and cooperation with Aborigines, so that those who persist in racist attitudes would feel themselves out of step with the community at large'. The means of attaining this were threefold: production of literature; research; and community education programs. Demonstrating something of Tatz's continued influence and legacy, Eggleston outlined plans for the provision of statistical bulletins on a variety of topics, beginning with an annual 'Survey of Race Relations in Australia' similar to that published by the South African Institute of Race Relations; an 'Education Bulletin', listing material suitable for primary and secondary students; 'study kits' suitable for different age groups; and a monthly journal specialising 'in lively and provocative articles dealing with race situations in other countries and commentary on development in Australia'. Second, Eggleston proposed the 'commissioning of special research projects to make the work of the Centre more effective'. In particular, she had in mind the 'speedy investigation' of 'crisis situations'; research undertaken at the request of Aboriginal groups'; and the evaluation of government programs being carried out in Aboriginal areas. Finally, Eggleston traced plans for the CRAA to play a role in 'devising and assisting in the carrying out of community education programs of all kinds to diminish prejudice'. In addition to courses delivered to police, nurses, teachers and doctors, she imagined the bringing together of small 'encounter' groups of Aborigines and whites, and the 'stimulation of interest among all sections of the community in racial questions'.

It was a vision in keeping with Tatz's original aims for the CRAA: it was 'action research', but on a much grander scale than had been possible to date. Expanding even further, the Board of the CRAA supported widening the scope of the proposed Race Relations Centre to encompass the problems of various ethnic minorities within a comparative international framework. Bryant, who met with the Vice Chancellor and several CRAA Board members in early October 1973, expressed strong interest in the proposal, but within days of the meeting had relinquished his portfolio, becoming Minister for the Capital Territory. Despite this and the reservations of some Board members who worried that the interests of Aborigines would become submerged in an enlarged unit, the proposal moved forward. Meetings were held with Al Grassby, Minister for Immigration and 'father of multiculturalism', to determine the likelihood of government support for a Race and Ethnic Relations Centre at Monash. Although, in the end, the proposal was dropped through lack of funds and interest, its conception nevertheless reveals a great deal about Eggleston's proactive and encompassing approach to Aboriginal research. Not all of her ideas bore fruit, but her desire to see the CRAA make a 'valuable contribution' drove her to continue testing and pushing the limits.

* * *

In the midst of Eggleston's expansion plans, the regular work of the CRAA continued. A residential seminar on 'Aborigines and the Law' was held at the Halls of Residence, Monash University, in July 1974. Opened by the federal Minister for Aboriginal Affairs, Senator Cavanagh, the seminar involved over one hundred participants and made forty-three separate recommendations, many radical, including: 'That all white executive or committee members of Aboriginal legal aid organisations resign or be removed; ... [and] That this seminar accepts the concept of black control of black affairs'. The latter resolution resounded with Eggleston who, in planning future residential seminars, insisted that '(i) no further strictly academic seminars be held and that (ii) research work in the Aboriginal field should be carried out by Aborigines, as much as possible'. In abandoning the idea of a future residential seminar on Aboriginal Arts, Eggleston explained that it would be better for such a seminar to 'emanate from Aborigines themselves'. More direct involvement of Aboriginal people in the daily operation and work of the CRAA was also sought.

The CRAA began employing Aboriginal research assistants at the end of 1973 when John Austin and Gary Murray were employed to conduct a study on the seasonal employment of Aborigines. A year later, Austin and Archie Roach were appointed to temporary research positions. They were followed by Steve Thorpe and Steve Aronson, who conducted research on legislation relating to Aborigines, and Laura Winslow who worked on the Resource Centre proposal. Bruce McGuiness, Austin and Lin Onus were co-opted onto the Centre's Board at around the same time. Eggleston firmly believed that 'participation by Aborigines in decision-making [was] even more important than consultation by whites with Aborigines'.

A major outcome of the Aboriginal Health Services seminar (held in 1972) was the setting up of an Aboriginal health journal administered by the Centre. The Health Services seminar had focused attention on the lack of 'means of communication between the various people working in the field of Aboriginal health', a situation 'exacerbated by the geographical isolation of many workers in the field'. Presented as a means of overcoming this problem, the idea of an Aboriginal health journal found ready support from the Department of Aboriginal Affairs which agreed to sponsor the journal via a special grant of $11,600. An editorial board headed by Dr Dobbin of the Department of Social and Preventative Medicine at Monash was named, and work commenced. However, the first issue, due out in February 1975, was delayed due to the difficulty of obtaining contributions.

At around the same time, Eggleston proposed that the CRAA take over production of a second periodical, *Newsletter on Aboriginal Affairs*, formerly produced by the Group for Information on Aboriginal Affairs in association with the Victorian Council of Churches. Three editions of the *Newsletter* had been printed, but the Group had insufficient funds to continue production. Eggleston was chairman and acting editor of the Group. Her proposal amounted to a plea for University sponsorship for the *Newsletter* which contained 'serious material not published elsewhere', emphasised 'Aboriginal viewpoints', reached libraries, teachers' colleges and individuals in Australia and abroad, and had the support of Aboriginal spokespeople such as Bruce McGuiness, an Aboriginal student at Monash. Eggleston explained that she planned to continue editing the *Newsletter* with the help of Laura Winslow and other Aboriginal research assistants at the Centre. The Board of the CRAA supported her proposal, but rather than publish two periodicals, it suggested combining the Aboriginal health journal, which was yet to appear, with the *Newsletter* and producing one publication. Renkin approved the plan to use the government's grant to produce a quarterly 'Aboriginal Affairs Review', the first issue of which would be on the subject of Aboriginal health, but the Department of Health objected. Having been part of the joint committee which had approved the original grant, it insisted on a focus on Aboriginal health. In the end, a single edition of *Aboriginal Issues: Health* (containing articles on the Aboriginal Medical Service at Redfern, government health polices, demographic data and statistics on infant mortality) was published in 1976 and, at the request of the Department of Aboriginal Affairs, the balance of the grant returned.

By the end of 1975, the CRAA was firmly 'established in relation to the Aboriginal community in Victoria' and, by virtue of its residential seminars, was 'widely known throughout Australia'. More than that, through the initiation of Black Australian Studies, the CRAA was vitally involved in the 'interpretation of the Aboriginal community to the white community in Australia'. Thanks largely to Eggleston's hard work and dedication, the Centre was providing a valuable public relations service, acting as a 'medium' between the university and the community. The time had come, the CRAA's Board believed, to augment these functions by the appointment of a full-time Director. The University agreed. While there was every hope that Eggleston would apply, and be successful, procedures had to be followed. Advertisements for a full-time director were placed in daily newspapers throughout the country, and in the Aboriginal journal *Identity*, with a closing date of 31 March 1976.

In December 1975 Lorna Lippman resigned her position of Research Officer at the CRAA. Two months later, Basil Hetzel resigned as Chairman of the CRAA's Board. By then, news of Eggleston's illness had broken. The new Chairman, Professor Louis Waller, recognising the Centre's firm ties with Aboriginal communities and government, its 'active involvement in day-to-day matters of great concern in the Aboriginal community', and its contributions to scholarly research, was committed to ensuring its maintenance and future development. The problem was the extent to which the activities of the Centre revolved around Eggleston (and, to a lesser extent, Lippman); almost all the Centre's activities were 'mounted under [Eggleston's] direction and guidance'. Eggleston died on 24 March 1976 – one week before applications for the position of full-time Director closed.

The social scientist Charles Rowley, reflecting on Eggleston's legacy, made much of the 'meticulous care with which she regarded and respected [the] opinions of young Aborigines'. Waller likewise called to mind her work with young Aboriginal people, especially students: 'quiet but determined, sensitive but firm, unobtrusive but deeply committed to what she saw as attainable goals, she listened, talked, gave advice, made suggestion, assembled and inspired'.

Monash's most famous Aboriginal alumnus, Professor Mick Dodson, was a student in the Law School during Eggleston's time as a teacher there. In the weeks before her death, while calmly arranging for the completion of many of her projects, she expressed concern for his and other Aboriginal students' welfare.

Elizabeth Eggleston Memorial Library

At the first meeting of the Board of the CRAA following Eggleston's death, it was agreed that an appeal for funds should be mounted to institute a suitable memorial. A number of proposals were discussed, but in end it was decided to focus on a project 'dear to Elizabeth's heart': the establishment of an Aboriginal Resource Centre. Accordingly, the Board agreed that Eggleston's 'library, which she had bequeathed to the Centre, should be made the basis of a continuing collection of books, documents (and perhaps other material such as tapes and films), dealing with Aboriginal Affairs'. The appeal was launched in July 1977, with a target set at $25,000. By March the following year the full amount had been realised. The appeal was supported by a range of people and organisations, both in Australia and overseas, including Eggleston's friends and family, her colleagues and members of the Aboriginal community. The Department of Aboriginal Affairs contributed $5000 to the appeal. The Elizabeth Eggleston Memorial Aboriginal Resource Centre (later Library) was opened in 1979. Rehoused several times in the intervening years, it is currently located on the 8th floor of the Menzies Building, an integral part of the Monash Indigenous Centre today.

Chapter 3

ABORIGINALISATION, 1977–97

Among the many changes ushered in by the election of Gough Whitlam's Australian Labor Party in 1972 was a commitment to restoring Aboriginal peoples' self-determination through a range of new government programs and increased levels of expenditure. Honoured by successive governments over the next two decades, this commitment resulted in the founding of Aboriginal legal and medical services managed by local Aboriginal communities, the inclusion of Aboriginal leaders in the processes of government, and other initiatives. As we saw in the previous chapter, the consequences of these developments for Monash's Centre for Research into Aboriginal Affairs were significant. Energised by an injection of funds, the CRAA embarked on a major program of expansion. However it was not until later, under Elizabeth Eggleston's successor, that the full impact of Whitlam's reform agenda was felt. Eggleston had hired casual Aboriginal research assistants and had sought Aboriginal participation in the CRAA's Board, but it took the appointment of an Aboriginal Director, Colin Bourke, to accelerate and name this process of Aboriginalisation within the University. Under Bourke, the CRAA embarked on a conscious program of Aboriginalisation that was part process and part mission. Applied to all aspects of the

CRAA's work, it gave the Centre a strong and positive focus that saw it grow in size and stature. This focus dissipated under subsequent Directors, such that when Bourke returned to the University in 1997, twenty years after his initial appointment, as a consultant engaged to review Monash's Aboriginal programs, he found cause to recommend a renewed focus on Aboriginalisation in line with University's then current focus on internationalisation. The Centre, once a leader in research on contemporary Aboriginal affairs, had become 'bereft of research activity'.

Colin Bourke: 'To Get As Many Aboriginal People As I Could'

Colin Bourke became the first full-time Director of the Centre for Research into Aboriginal Affairs in 1977. He was also the first Aboriginal Director. A teacher with the Victorian Education Department, Bourke was vice-principal at Keon Park Primary School at the time of his appointment. His acceptance of the fixed-term two-year appointment was conditional upon the Education Department consenting to a secondment arrangement, which it did. In 1975, two years before his secondment, Bourke had served as Supervisor of Aboriginal Education with the Special Services Division of the Education Department. Convinced that Aboriginal education was composed of 'two distinguishable but dependent parts', namely 'education of Aborigines, and education of the non-Aboriginal community about Aborigines', Bourke came to the CRAA determined to 'assist in the development of both aspects'. He knew the challenge that faced him, but was 'devoted to the fulfillment of the hopes and aspirations of the Aboriginal people'. One of his referees, Eric Willmot, described him, pointedly, as a member of the 'new group of emergent Aboriginal professionals whose effect on the course of Aboriginal destiny is likely to be a significant event in Australian history'.

A father of four, Bourke was accustomed to the pressures of a busy life. Born in Sunshine, Victoria, he commenced work with the Victorian Education Department in 1955, moving through the ranks from classroom assistant to principal. He became a teacher, he recalled, because of what his father told him about the Depression: 'everybody got sacked, [but] teachers were still employed ... if you want security, be a teacher'. Bourke wanted security, but he had other ambitions. His dream was to teach the next generation of teachers. Having always harboured a desire to go to university, in 1968 he decided to 'have a crack at doing a degree'. Knocked back on account of his low matriculation grade, he enrolled in a correspondence course, improved his grade and was accepted to the University of Melbourne the next year, graduating with a Bachelor of Commerce in 1974, and a Bachelor of Education in 1976.

Bourke knew about the CRAA and its work under Colin Tatz and Elizabeth Eggleston, but he was not looking for a job. It was Richard Eggleston, Chancellor of Monash and Elizabeth's father, who alerted him to the position: '[he] rang me up and he said "a position is vacant, will you apply for it?"' Within weeks of commencing at Monash, the Commonwealth Department of Education requested permission to appoint Bourke to the National Aboriginal Education Committee (NAEC), a new organisation consisting solely of Aboriginal members whose purpose was to advise government and other authorities on the educational needs of Aboriginal people from pre-school to university. Informed that Bourke's membership of the NAEC would entail attendance at three or four meetings per year, the University agreed. A sign of the times, Bourke's involvement in the NAEC and other Aboriginal organisations, both government and community, was a feature of his directorship which saw an increasingly politicised Aboriginal perspective brought to bear upon the Centre's work.

Bourke's first two years as Director of the CRAA were characterised by continuity and change. The Centre continued to 'undertake and stimulate research and to examine the problems Aborigines have in living in a predominantly white society with the aim of helping bring about an improvement in that situation'. However, emphasis was increasingly placed on the latter aspect (i.e. improving 'the situation of the indigenous people of this country'). The practice of employing Aboriginal staff, commenced during Eggleston's time, also continued. What changed was the articulation and consciousness of this as 'Aboriginalisation'. In his first Director's report, having completed nearly eight months in the role, Bourke wrote that the Centre had 'undergone a degree of Aboriginalisation in relation to staff and research activities following the appointment of an Aboriginal Director'. In his second report, he noted that this 'Aboriginalisation … [had] continued with respect to personnel, philosophy and activities'. What also changed was the size and location of the Centre. In May 1977 the Centre moved from the Law School to the fourth floor of the Education building where it occupied three rooms. By the end of the following year, it occupied five rooms, but was still overcrowded.

The Centre grew rapidly under Bourke, largely as a result of his ability to extract funds from various sources and his commitment to employing Aboriginal people. As Professor Louis Waller, Chairman of the CRAA's Board, related to Basil Hetzel, former Chairman of the Board:

> [Bourke] is energetic, and particularly able in the preparation of proposals for, and the pursuit of, grants from government and semi-government bodies. This, coupled with a regular policy of employing, as much as possible, young Aborigines as clerical staff and research assistants, has made the Centre a contributor, in a small way, to [Aboriginal] employment in this part of Melbourne.

During 1977 funds were received from the Department of Aboriginal Affairs to employ several Aboriginal people: Wayne Atkinson and Colin Johnson were appointed as research assistants, and two temporary clerical assistants, Noretta Knight and Carolin Martin, were appointed among others. Further funds for a short-term research project conducted by Kevin Gilbert were also received. 'All these new members of staff', Bourke proudly reported, 'are Aborigines'.

Many of the Aboriginal staff employed by the Centre under Bourke became influential members of the Aboriginal community: Atkinson completed a Bachelor of Arts and PhD at La Trobe University, worked extensively in Indigenous affairs and played a leading role in Yorta Yorta land and heritage matters; Johnson, also known as Mudrooroo Narogin, became a well-known, if somewhat controversial novelist, poet and playwright; Knight worked for the Aboriginal Development Commission in Canberra; and Martin worked as a senior policy adviser for the Victorian State Government Departments of Education and Human Services before being appointed Manager, Bunjilaka Aboriginal Cultural Centre at Museum Victoria. Gilbert, who played a leading role in the 1972 Tent Embassy demonstration, was already an accomplished playwright at the time of his appointment. In 1988 he was awarded the Human Rights and Equal Opportunity Commission's Human Rights Award for Literature, but he returned the medal citing the ongoing injustice and suffering of his people.

The funding of the Centre during 1977 and 1978 continued the pattern set in earlier years. The University paid the salaries of the Director and the secretary and all other funds had to be found from other sources. That the employment of Aboriginal people at the Centre was only possible through 'special Department of Aboriginal Affairs funding' was a source of frustration and concern to Bourke. Skilled in the art of grant writing he may have been, but Bourke found the process of applying for funds 'an extremely arduous task'. He concluded his first Director's report with the familiar lament that much of the Centre's work was devoted towards obtaining funds 'in order to carry on the work of the Centre'. A partial solution was found in 1978 when the Department of Employment and Industrial Relations (later the Department of Employment and Youth Affairs) agreed to classify the CRAA as a Training Centre for Aborigines under the National Employment Strategy for Aborigines, part of the National Employment and Training (NEAT) scheme. This meant that the Department paid 100 percent of the wages and on-costs of Aboriginal people employed as trainees at the Centre. Most of the training positions were short-term which meant the Centre continually had new trainees. Even though this lessened its overall efficiency, so important was the CRAA's role as an employer of Aboriginal people that Bourke sought recognition of this as one of the its main functions.

The CRAA's tripartite purpose, 'research, resource and teaching', was enlarged to include 'employment' in 1978. The three original functions were also sharpened as a result of the Centre's Aboriginalisation. The CRAA continued to function as a resource centre (despite the lack of suitable accommodation or funding) with Bourke noting a 'dramatic' increase in the 'number of Aboriginal people visiting the Centre and using its resources'. Anticipating that 'this trend would continue', Bourke hoped that 'eventually the Aboriginal Organisations [would] use the resources of the Centre in preparing their submissions to Government and other funding bodies'. Indeed, this was an important part of his vision for the Centre's future — that it would become a central repository of information and hub of activities for Aboriginal people and their organisations in greater Melbourne. During 1977 the Centre's resources were expanded to include recordings of the Black Studies lectures that recommenced that year (see below). An additional resource was found among the small number of Aboriginal students enrolled at Monash; the Centre encouraged them to undertake speaking engagements at local schools.

In 1978 the Centre employed a young Aboriginal woman and trainee librarian, Wendy Carter, on a part-time basis to catalogue and organise the large body of resource material which, that year, was moved to a dedicated room attached to the office of the Centre's secretary. The Elizabeth Eggleston Memorial Aboriginal Resource Centre was opened in August, though it took another year before it was fully functioning. By the end of 1980 the CRAA was employing two Aboriginal trainee library technicians to work in the Resource Centre which now held 'over six hundred monograph titles, ninety periodical titles, about two thousand pamphlet titles, newspaper clippings, theses, audio tapes, video tapes, annual reports of Aboriginal organisations, Australian Bureau of Statistics publications, Aboriginal Research Centre reports and publications, seminar reports, maps, Acts and Bills, and official government Hansards'.

The Aboriginalisation of the Centre was also felt in the area of research. Rather than continuing to respond only (or mainly) to the 'needs of those groups who have the finance and resources to commission research', Bourke sought to employ Aboriginal trainee research assistants who could 'react to the research needs of the Aboriginal community'. This was not to deny or downplay the significance of commissioned research; rather, it was to highlight the potential of Aboriginal-led *and* initiated research. Although most of the research conducted by the CRAA continued to be of the former kind, increasingly it was conducted by Aboriginal researchers. In 1977 the Victorian Education Department commissioned research on Aboriginal education. Worked on by several members of the CRAA, including Colin Johnson, Wayne Atkinson and Bourke, the resulting twenty-page booklet, *Aboriginal Educational Services in Victoria*, provided a comprehensive overview of Commonwealth and State education services, Aboriginal administered services, and services provided by other organisations including Monash University, the University of Melbourne, Save the Children Fund, and the Master Plumbers Association. Copies were sent to every school in Victoria and efforts were made to distribute the booklet to all Aboriginal families in Victoria.

During 1977 the Education Research and Development Committee, an advisory committee to the Commonwealth Minister for Education, invited Bourke to make an assessment of the bilingual education programs being offered to Aboriginal people around Australia. Most of the research was conducted during 1978; the report was completed in 1979. Other research projects conducted during 1978 included: an Aboriginal history of Tasmania by Colin Johnson funded by the Aboriginal Arts Board; a study of the history of Cummerragunja by Wayne Atkinson, paid for by the Australian Institute for Aboriginal Studies; a ten-week survey regarding the possibility of introducing an Aboriginal language into Victorian schools underwritten the Victorian Education Department; and a two-month study of the effectiveness of welfare services for Victorian Aboriginal people funded by Victorian Council of Social Services. The latter two projects were undertaken by Eve Fesl, future Director of the CRAA.

The CRAA hosted two conferences and an art exhibition during 1978. The first conference, held in May at the Monash Halls of Residence, considered the 'Future of the South-Eastern Australian Aborigines'. Attended by more than eighty Aboriginal people, Bourke remarked that he thought 'it could easily rank as a major achievement in Aboriginal Affairs'. The second conference, on Aboriginal unemployment, was held at the Victorian Aborigines Advancement League (VAAL) office in Northcote. Well attended by Aboriginal people and representatives of various State and Commonwealth Departments, the views expressed found a ready ear in the recently established National Aboriginal Employment Development Committee, of which Bourke was a member. In December nine Milingimbi artists and performers from Arnhem Land (Northern Territory) were brought to Monash for a two-weeks art exhibition and workshop. The grounds at Marist College were transformed into a traditional-type setting where paintings, carvings, weapons, musical instruments and weavings were exhibited and sold, and demonstrations held. Over 2000 people attended the exhibition and participated in the workshops.

The Aboriginalisation of the Centre continued in the area of teaching. The 'Black Australian Studies' course pioneered by Eggleston in 1974 and 1975 (see Chapter 2) recommenced as a not-for-credit course in 1977. Initially scheduled on Tuesday evenings, the year-long course attracted a modest twenty to thirty participants. However, following the decision to repeat the evening lecture at lunchtime, the numbers attending greatly increased. Notable speakers, such as Charles Perkins, Margaret Valadian, and Kath Walker commanded audiences of up to ninety people at lunchtime. Bourke was especially pleased at the number of Aboriginal students and community members attending the lectures. He estimated that half or more of the audience at Perkins' lecture was Aboriginal. Towards the end of 1977, at the request of the Aboriginal Liaison Officer at the University of Melbourne, Eleanor Koumalatsos, the evening lecture was moved to the University of Melbourne. Bourke's agreement signaled his hope of increasing 'the dissemination of Aboriginal studies' to audiences in central Melbourne, especially Aboriginal people. The course continued to be taught at both universities under the auspices of the CRAA in 1978–1981.

The list of proposed speakers for Black Studies in 1978 was a veritable who's who of notable Aboriginal people: Galarrwuy Yunupingu, Marcia Langton, Lois O'Donoghue, John Newfong, Charles Perkins, Bruce McGuiness, and Chicka Dixon were just some of the Aboriginal speakers the Centre hoped to secure. This was an important point of difference between the Centre's Black Studies course and similar courses offered at other tertiary institutions. As Bourke noted in his application for accreditation in 1978, the course not only examined issues 'from the Aboriginal perspective', but imparted 'first-hand information' on Aboriginal issues by Aboriginal people. Later, reflecting on the significance of this, he explained that he felt there were too many non-Aboriginal people talking about Aboriginal people, and too few Aboriginal people 'giving their views of what Aboriginal people think or want … If you're going to have someone talk about land rights, why not get someone who is leading the land rights push?' To Bourke, it did not matter that the guest lecturers were 'a bit rough around the edges'. What mattered was hearing 'Aboriginal voices ... giving the other side of the story which had never [before] been listened to'.

Waller, writing in support of Bourke's application for accreditation for Black Studies, advised the Dean of the Faculty of Arts, Professor J.D. Legge, that offering such a course 'would increase the stature of Aborigines, and in doing so, make a positive contribution to improving race relations in this country'. Although the University eventually agreed, initially the answer was 'no'. The course was considered 'not academic' enough, Bourke explained: 'the Dean said no ... you haven't got a lecturer in charge, you haven't got a syllabus and [so on]'. Bourke met the Dean's objections: 'we started knocking them off, one by one, and in the end we got our accreditation'. As well as Black Studies, during 1978 Bourke lectured on Aboriginal education to Bachelor of Education students at Monash, and Diploma of Education students at various teachers colleges; the Centre combined with the Linguistics Department to offer a beginners course in Pitjantjatjara; and Fesl conducted weekly classes in Aboriginal Studies at the Ferntree Gully Women's Educational Co-operative.

Bourke's goal was to 'get as many Aboriginal people as he could' involved in all aspects of the Centre's work, including its Board. During Eggleston's time, efforts had been made to recruit Aboriginal Board members, but with limited success. This was escalated under Bourke who, at the end of his first year as Director, nominated three new Aboriginal Board members: Eleanor Koumalatsos (Aboriginal Liaison Office, University of Melbourne), Penny Maxwell (administrative secretary, Victorian Aboriginal Co-operative), and Reg Blow

From left: Colin Bourke, Reg Blow, Ian Viner (Minister for Aboriginal Affairs), Professor Ray Martin, Proffesor Louis Waller
Source: Monash Archives

(administrator, Dandenong and District Co-operative). All three joined the Board in 1978. Three years later half of the Board were Aboriginal: in Bourke's view, having 'membership of an Aboriginal Research Centre Board within a University consisting of equal proportions of University staff members and Aborigines' was 'a very satisfactory situation'.

The question of whether Bourke would return to teaching at the end of his period of secondment was resolved with his acceptance of a tenured position as Director of the CRAA at the end of 1978. With security and experience came the freedom and desire to implement greater change. Bourke noted in January 1979 that 'the objectives of the Centre', having changed little since 1964, were 'to be reviewed'.

First on the list was the Centre's relationship with the Australian Institute of Aboriginal Studies (AIAS) in Canberra. The CRAA's relationship with the AIAS had always been strained, largely as a result of the founding Director, Colin Tatz's open disdain for the AIAS's focus on the past. In 1978 the AIAS funded a pilot project on the history of Cummeragunja and this prompted Bourke to reflect that the CRAA had 'no knowledge of the materials they [the AIAS] have available on the Victorian Aborigines'. Discussions with the AIAS Principal, Peter Ucko, resulted in the AIAS funding a researcher from the CRAA to compile a bibliography of their holdings on Victoria. Colin Johnson undertook the task. Seeking to further improve the Centre's relationship with the AIAS, Bourke joined several AIAS sub-committees: the Education, Publications, and Aboriginal and Torres Strait Islander Advisory Committees. During 1979 Ucko and a Senior Research Fellow, Alex Barlow, visited the CRAA.

Bourke recognised the importance of committee work for building and maintaining the Centre's profile. As well as serving on the AIAS committees, the National Aboriginal Education Committee, and the National Aboriginal Employment Development Committee, Bourke served on the Victorian Aboriginal Education Consultative Group, and the Victorian In-Service Education Committee Aboriginal Sub-Committee. The proliferation of Aboriginal committees during this period pointed to the professionalisation and bureaucratisation of the struggle for justice for Aboriginal people. It also pointed to the greater amount of government funding available for Aboriginal organisations. The Department for Aboriginal Affairs increased its allocation to the Centre by fifty percent in the 1978–79 financial year, bringing the total received to $27,000. This was increased the following year to $40,700. Funding for specific research projects was also received from other government bodies, including: the Commonwealth Department of Education, the Department of Community Welfare, and the Victorian Education Department. The latter department funded the Bandjalang Language Program. Building on the Aboriginal language survey conducted the previous year, the CRAA in conjunction with the Victorian Aboriginal Education Consultative Group, brought the Bandjalang language into Warnnambool West and Bell Primary Schools on a trial basis in 1979. The program, which attracted considerable media attention, was continued the following year.

Like Tatz and Eggleston before him, Bourke maintained a good relationship with the Victorian Aborigines Advancement League. In 1979, in the face of falling membership, Bourke called on the embattled League 'to define its role and direction in Aboriginal affairs for the future'. Subsequently, a two-day seminar was held at Monash 'aimed at crystallising [the VAAL's] future role and areas of responsibility in Aboriginal Affairs'. Requests from other Aboriginal organisations and individuals for joint research projects were received from the Victorian Aboriginal Cooperative, the Victorian Aboriginal Child Care Agency, and Robert (Bobby) Merritt, author of *Cake Man* (1975). The most ambitious project was that proposed by the Aboriginal Child Care Agency. It wanted to develop a research project that would examine what happened to Aboriginal children in Victoria from 1939–79, focusing on the role of government agencies involved in the placement of Aboriginal children. This followed the 'First Aboriginal Child Survival Seminar' convened by the Aboriginal Child Care Agency in Melbourne in April 1979. Representing as they did the 'research needs of the Aboriginal community', these requests received Bourke's full support. He managed to secure funding from the AIAS for the Victorian Aboriginal Cooperative's joint project on Aboriginal housing needs in Victoria, and the Department of Aboriginal Affairs paid for a pilot survey on the effects of prisons on Aborigines in New South Wales undertaken by Merritt, but the project on Aboriginal children was not pursued. Such a topic would, in years to come, assume critical importance in understanding the disadvantaged state of Aboriginal people; in 1979, however, appreciation of the nature and extent of Aboriginal child removal was still in its infancy.

In recognition of the Centre's Aboriginalisation, Bourke suggested changing its name to a title that more readily identified its changed outlook and focus. In July 1979, the Centre for Research into Aboriginal Affairs became the Aboriginal Research Centre. Personally, Bourke preferred MARC, the Monash Aboriginal Research Centre, but the Board opted for ARC. At its November meeting the ARC Board considered a document prepared by the Director proposing the admission of Aboriginal students to Monash University under a revised special admissions scheme. Speaking to the document, Bourke informed the Board that there were significant numbers 'of Aborigines wishing to undertake university courses' who had little chance of gaining entry in the normal way or under the existing special admissions scheme. Under the existing scheme, early school leavers and other applicants were required to sit and achieve a minimum level of performance in a general test of scholastic aptitude. Rather than subject Aboriginal candidates to a culturally specific aptitude test, the Board of the ARC agreed that steps should be taken to establish more appropriate avenues for entry. Several alternatives were considered. In the end the Board resolved to recommend that the relevant University regulations be altered to enable Aborigines seeking admission to the University to be considered for selection by a special committee convened by the ARC. While not resulting in any immediate change, this decision helped to pave the way for future change.

With Colin Johnson and anthropologist Isobel White, Bourke co-wrote *Before The Invasion: Aboriginal Life to 1788*, an overview of pre-contact Aboriginal life aimed at school children, during 1979. The publisher, Oxford University Press, did not believe 'that two Aboriginal people could write a book on their own': they got White involved, Bourke recalled, and while she was great to work with, their lack of faith was galling.

The year 1979 was also when 'Aboriginal Studies', formerly 'Black Australian Studies', was first offered as a course for credit in the Faculty of Arts. Forty students enrolled and Eve Fesl, a Monash graduate with an honours degree in sociology, was employed as Senior Tutor. One of the conditions of accreditation, Fesl, who had previously worked as a research assistant and secretary in the Centre, was to provide continuity in a course that was taught by a different guest lecturer each week. Students surveyed at the conclusion of the course reported learning not only a 'great deal of knowledge about Aboriginal culture', but gaining 'a fresh perspective on their own society and its value systems' as a result. The course was taught again in 1980. Some thirty students enrolled and, as in previous years, the lectures were also open to the public.

The Faculty of Arts reviewed the course in 1979 and 1980. The second review resulted in a 'flood of letters' from concerned students protesting – 'sometimes in somewhat offensive terms' – against what they saw as the Faculty's negative attitude to the course. Most of the letter writers complained that the course only lasted one year, however some alluded to concerns, raised in the review, about the course's academic standards. One letter, addressed to the Vice Chancellor, expressed 'anger and disgust' at the university's inability to 'see when a course is of importance and value to an individual and his society'. The student's tirade concluded with an open challenge to the Vice Chancellor to enroll in the course:

> If the course appears less academic to you than another subject, it is because you refuse to let it be by limiting the amount of time allowed to cover an area that has a history of 60,000 years in Australia. If you still consider the course is not academic enough, then I feel you should reevaluate the standards of education in this University ... If still you are not convinced, I suggest you enroll in the course for 1981 ... to get an understanding of the people we are studying and ... hearing their interpretation of their own affairs.

The university registrar, J.D. Butchart, doubted whether any of the students had actually seen the review. Instead, it seemed they 'had been fed some of the comments' and 'encouraged to write as part of a propaganda exercise'. The Dean of Arts, J.D. Legge agreed that the letters were probably 'inspired', but that did not concern him. What worried him was that 'not one of the letters' was 'correctly informed about the facts of the case', including 'the possibility of the Faculty giving additional money to the course next year'. Legge advised Bourke to inform his students 'that a campaign as ill-informed as this one [was] likely to be counter-productive'. The main suggestion arising from the review was that a series of lectures be given by one visiting lecturer to promote continuity and depth, for which the Faculty of Arts agreed to provide additional funds. In 1981, Eric Willmott, new Principal of the AIAS, was engaged to deliver four lectures.

MAKING A DIFFERENCE

By then Bourke had resigned. In his final Director's report, Bourke took aim at the University for failing to provide secure funding: 'Despite its use of many funding sources the Centre is always experiencing difficulty in making ends meet', he reproached. By way of example, he relayed how he had had to refrain from appointing a clerical assistant during 1980 so that funds earmarked for that role could be reallocated to pay the senior tutor whose work was essential for the Aboriginal Studies course. He made it clear that the 'level of funding provided at present [was] seriously hindering the development of the Centre'. The present accommodation was also inadequate: 'The Centre has serious overcrowding problems', Bourke complained. He estimated that an additional sixteen offices and purpose built resource centre and language laboratory were required. But these were matters for his successor to pursue.

Bourke left the university in March 1981 to take up a position as General Manager of the recently created Aboriginal Development Commission. He and his new wife Eleanor (formerly Koumalatsos), an ARC Board member (and future Director of the Centre), were farewelled at a cocktail party attended by the Chancellor, Deputy-Chancellor, Vice Chancellor, ARC Board members, Monash staff, and Aboriginal community leaders. On his last day of work Bourke was interviewed by Professor Merle Ricklefs, a recent appointee in the History Department, who wanted to know what could be done to increase the number of Aboriginal students at Monash. Not through lack of trying, Bourke had not managed to Aboriginalise the student-body. Busy packing his office, Bourke replied: 'what you need is a bridging course'. Bourke's successor, Eve Fesl worked with Ricklefs to establish the Monash Orientation Scheme for Aborigines (see chapter 4), a path-breaking initiative that saw the number of

Aboriginal students enrolled at Monash grow from one in 1983 to fifty-four by 1991.

Eve Fesl: 'A Somewhat Fearsome Reputation'

Eve Fesl was appointed Acting Director of the Aboriginal Research Centre in 1981, and was confirmed as Director by the end of that year. Fesl had been involved in every aspect of the Centre's operation since her employment as a casual research assistant in 1977. As Bourke's secretary in 1978, she was instrumental in developing the administrative machinery that enabled the Centre to become a training facility for Aboriginal people. The following year she became senior tutor in Aboriginal Studies. In 1980 she travelled as a representative of the ARC to Perpignan in the south of France where she attended the inaugural conference of the *'La Societe Francaise Pour La Promotion De La Culture Des Aborigines Australiens'*. By 1981 Fesl was, in her own words, 'fully conversant with the functioning of the Centre', and was 'acquainted with most of the clients and persons involved in the Centre's business'. She was also intimately familiar with the University itself, having been a student there since 1974.

Born in Queensland in 1930, Fesl's ancestors were Gubbi Gubbi and Yiman peoples. Excelling in sport, she moved to Melbourne in 1956, her sights set on making the Olympic discus team, but she was not selected. She enrolled in night school, eventually matriculating with the state's highest mark in German. This led to her being invited to enter the German Department at Monash University. She ended up studying anthropology, sociology and linguistics, graduating with a Bachelor of Arts with honours in 1978. At the time of her appointment as Director of the Aboriginal Research Centre, she was completing a Master of Arts thesis on the Aboriginal languages of Gippsland. Fesl, as reported in the *Sun*, shattered 'any bigot's stereotype of an Aboriginal'; she was 'gracious, elegant, accomplished and sophisticated'; she was also extremely hard working, averaging seventy hours per week. She had strong views on a range of social issues and stood up for what she believed in: she was pro-environment and anti-freeways; she served as president of the Save the Kangaroo Committee; and, with her husband, showed her support for the ideal of Zero Population Growth by choosing to remain childless.

Within a month of Bourke's departure, Fesl revealed herself to be a leader with a clear vision for the Centre's future. Based on her understanding of the needs of the Aboriginal community, as well as her 'perception of the direction in which the Centre is heading', she identified the ARC's future priorities: 1. Research; 2. Aboriginal Studies; 3. Bandjalang Language Program. In her first report as Acting Director, Fesl stipulated that any future funding would be allocated on a priority basis 'in line with the above hierarchy'. Her approach to management was very hands-on; she had oversight of all the Centre's research and teaching projects and was not averse to admonishing those whose work failed to reach acceptable standards. She had no qualms, for example, about calling-out an Aboriginal researcher whose work – or rather lack thereof – had 'become a source of embarrassment to the Centre'. Maintaining a tight control over the Centre's budget, Fesl proudly reported at the end of her first year in the job that the ARC was functioning within its budget. She approached the Department of Aboriginal Affairs not as supplicant, but as a 'grateful' recipient of its 'continued financial support'. She was also 'grateful' to Monash University for its 'practical support' and encouragement.

Director of the ARC for over a decade, from 1981 to 1993, Fesl oversaw a tumultuous period in the Centre's history. Once a lone voice on contemporary Aboriginal Affairs, the Centre's point of difference had dissipated with the growth of Aboriginal-led organisations during the 1970s. In the two decades since the Centre's establishment, much had changed in Aboriginal Affairs; legal forms of discrimination against Aboriginal people had been removed from the statute books, and Aboriginal peoples' access to education, employment, health-care, housing, legal and other essential services had improved. The steadily increasing number of students taking Aboriginal Studies at Monash, and high number of enquiries received by the ARC for information and advice about Aboriginal issues suggested that community attitudes were also changing. Yet, there was still work to be done.

Where Bourke's research interests and expertise lay in education, Fesl's lay in linguistics; appropriately the Centre's focus shifted in line with the new Director's expertise. Fesl had been employed as a research assistant in the late 1970s working on a project commissioned by the Victorian Aboriginal Education Consultative Group on the feasibility of introducing an Aboriginal language into Victorian schools. The outcome, as described above, was a trial of the Bandjalang language at two primary schools in 1980. Bandjalang was spoken by Aboriginal people in the north of New South Wales. Its introduction into Victorian schools was recommended by Fesl because she felt that no Victorian Aboriginal languages could be revived, and it was the closest – geographically speaking – Aboriginal language still in daily use.

In March 1981 Fesl escorted seven teachers and teacher-aides to the areas around Lismore where the Bandjalang language was spoken. The aim of the visit was to help the teachers obtain a feel for the language through greater understanding of the cultural background and atmosphere out of which the language arose. This was important, Fesl explained, because 'otherwise it would be like someone trying to teach the French word and meaning for bread when they did not know that the first task for the day of every French child is to go and collect the family's bread-sticks'. Following the visit, which attracted positive publicity for the Centre, Aboriginal elders in the Lismore area invited Fesl to return to help establish a Bandjalang language program in schools in their area. That year Bandjalang was taught into four Victorian schools (Warrnambool West, Bell Primary, Preston Technical and Robinvale Primary), and an adult class was planned. Plans were also made for the introduction of Walpiri, a 'strongly traditional language' spoken by Aboriginal people north and west of Alice Springs. The distinction Fesl drew between Walpiri and Bandjalang was instructive. She explained that 'unlike Bandjalang ... [Walpiri was] spoken by Aboriginal people living a different lifestyle to Victorian Aboriginal people'. The point of teaching Walpiri was thus to give Aboriginal students an 'opportunity to look at a culture which, in many respects, may resemble that of their forebears'. By 1985 the second stage of the Bandjalang language program had been successfully trialed and the production of books suitable for both adults and children was underway.

Another major project, 'Personal Development Through Literacy', commenced in 1981 with the appointment of three Aboriginal community researchers, one each in Fitzroy (Melbourne), Drouin (Victoria), and Bourke (New South Wales), whose task was to collect data and carry out observations in their own communities. The results, compiled by Fesl, were published in 1982 as *Bala Bala: Some Literacy and Educational Perceptions of Three Aboriginal Communities*.

The establishment of MOSA, described in the following chapter, occupied a considerable amount of Fesl's time during 1982–83. Having been a student at Monash in the 1970s herself, she knew first hand 'the kind of isolation white students could never know'. She recalled stumbling 'blindly through her first years studying German without a text book, [only] to discover the next year that the book was available from the university'. Once MOSA was established, Fesl's involvement in the bridging course was marginal. MOSA and the ARC were separate entities: 'completely separate', according to Ricklefs, MOSA's co-founder. In the initial proposal for the establishment of the bridging course, Ricklefs explained that while there should be 'close and cordial contact between the orientation year program and the Aboriginal Research Centre', the two programs should 'be kept separate in an institutional sense'. Some overlapping of membership between the Board of the ARC and the MOSA Committee was envisaged, but they were not to be housed together or thought of as sharing a purpose, 'the two programs' general aims and responsibilities [being] rather different'. No-one objected to this distinction.

During the mid 1980s the ARC was involved in a national review of Aboriginal employment and training programs, funded by the Department of Employment and Industrial Relations, and was awarded a Community Education Program grant to train Aboriginal women in the identification, preparation and use of Aboriginal plant foods of Victoria. Increasingly, the Centre was called upon to research and write submissions for various government agencies and departments, and more and more time was spent responding to requests for information and advice. Accompanied by an explosion in demand for 'competent Aboriginal speakers or lecturers', the

Centre found it necessary 'to confine itself to meeting the needs ... of universities ... and other institutions of higher education and national conferences of importance'.

Indicative of the divisive nature of some of its work, as well as the growth of splinter groups of Aboriginal activists within society, during 1984 and 1985 strong criticism was leveled at the Director and the Centre from the Victorian Aborigines Advancement League (VAAL) and from individual members of the Victorian Aboriginal community for failing 'to work for the good of all'. The controversy began as a power struggle within the VAAL that culminated in legal proceedings initiated by Fesl and others. Prior to the League's AGM in 1984, the League's management committee had sought to prevent a takeover by limiting voting rights. Fesl and her co-plaintiffs wanted the management committee to abide by the principles of community control and open membership on which the League had been founded. The VAAL's Director (and future Centre Director), Sharon Firebrace, sought to have Fesl sacked, but Monash's Chancellor, Sir George Lush was unmoved: 'This University will not dismiss a member of its staff merely because a body outside the University expresses opinions adverse to such a member'.

A formidable and impressive character, by 1985 Fesl's reputation for standing up for what she believed in was well known. A visiting professor from the University of Western Australia, Robert Tonkinson, remarked following lunch with Fesl that he now understood why she had 'a somewhat fearsome reputation': after battling 'away on several topics', they parted cordially, their 'humour and respective positions intact'. Fesl completed her Master of Arts thesis in 1986 and commenced work on a PhD under the supervision of Professor Michael Clyne. An internationally celebrated socio-

Dr Eve Fesl with Vice Chancellor Professor Mal Logan after being awarded her doctorate
Source: Monash Archives
Photographer: Richard Crompton

linguist, Clyne worked mainly in the areas of bilingualism and language maintenance. Guided by Clyne, Fesl completed her doctoral dissertation in less than three years. One of the first Aboriginal people to be awarded a doctorate, and the first at Monash, Fesl's thesis examined the use of English as a tool of oppression. Arguing that the 'English language was used to conceal a slave trade in Australia', she claimed in interviews following the award of her doctorate that both her parents were slaves: 'In every Koori family there were slaves'.

The name 'Koori' or 'Koorie', meaning 'our people', began being openly and widely used by Aboriginal people in south-eastern Australia during the 1970s and 1980s. Before then Koori had been a semi-secret word used among Aboriginal people themselves but not generally known by outsiders. Drawing on the research for her thesis, towards the end of 1988 Fesl suggested that the name of the Centre be changed to the 'Koorie Research Centre'. There were several reasons why such a change was desirable, according to Fesl, but the most significant related to the connotations of the terms 'Aboriginal' and 'Koorie'. She explained that:

> The word 'Aborigine' is a noun which refers to an indigenous group of any country. It is a term which the English first used when they invaded Australia. As a name of a group of people it is non-descriptive, placing the native peoples of Australia into a hodge-podge of peoples, without giving them a named identity ... Furthermore, the term 'Aboriginal' often is felt to have derogatory connotations, associated from the 19th century with pejorative terms such as 'primitive', 'savage', 'barbaric', etc.

Koorie, on the other hand, was the name that the 'indigenous peoples of Victoria call themselves'. Fesl argued that is was therefore 'appropriate that a Centre [such as the ARC], situated in Victoria, should adopt a name more relevant to the people of this state rather than using the identity-less, indeed, often pejorative, term 'Aboriginal'.

The Board of the ARC was supportive of Fesl's request and the timing seemed right. At least one member of the ARC's Board, Dr B.M. Bullivant, objected to the proposal. Historian Bruce Knox, a member of the Professorial Board, also objected. Knox felt that the term 'Koori' narrowed the definition of the Centre 'very severely'. Whereas the present title of the Centre reflected the purpose of its establishment, the new title proclaimed 'that only studies deriving from, or affecting, the Aboriginal people of south-eastern Australia' would be undertaken. 'Koori', he stressed, 'is an exclusive term and needs to be used with discretion'. His objections were noted but overruled. As part of Monash' response to the Bicentenary, the Centre's name was changed in 1989.

'1988 and All That'

In recognition of her efforts to preserve and promote Aboriginal culture and languages, as well as her service to the development of multiculturalism, Fesl was made a Member of the Order of Australia in 1988. Like many Aboriginal people, Fesl saw the Bicentenary as an occasion 'not to celebrate, but for Australia to face its history. Until they face it, we won't have harmony', she declared. Reflecting a growing mood of Aboriginal assertiveness, especially in the area of Aboriginal history, Fesl called on white Australians to acknowledge the violence of the frontier and 'honour the Kooris who died in atrocities'. She also wanted acknowledgment of the history of Aboriginal child removal. The burgeoning awareness of the 'stolen generations' that followed in the wake of Peter Read's research in the early 1980s and subsequent establishment of Link-Up, prompted Fesl to note that many removed children were looking for their parents in the bicentennial year: 'What do you say to the woman who traced her mother too late, two years after she died? Celebrate?'

The Bicentennial year was an extremely busy one at the Centre, all staff taking the opportunity to disseminate information on Aboriginal matters while interest was high. Fesl personally delivered thirty papers to community groups and conferences, and wrote numerous articles. Interviewed by the *Herald* on the eve of the Bicentennial year, Fesl described her goal for 1988: 'it is to have the principle accepted that by 1990 there will be core units of Aboriginal studies in teaching courses, and special places reserved for Koori lecturers at training colleges'. Fesl wanted research conducted into teachers attitudes towards children of non-English speaking backgrounds: 'You have to wipe out racist attitudes and practices in schools and that depends on having good anti-racist teachers', she explained. Since Bourke's time the Centre had run electives in the Education Department at Monash, seeking to ensure that new teachers entering the school system were 'conversant with Aboriginal culture/language and the effects of the institutional clash on Aboriginal students'. Student teachers were trained 'in the selection of non-racist literature and curricula and methods of "unlearning stereotypes" of Aboriginal people and culture'. Fesl's larger dream was to establish 'our own colleges' where Aboriginal children could go from 'pre-school to HSC level' and experience 'no racism'. At such places, she explained: 'You could ensure the curricula did not include negative things ... like teaching kids Captain Cook discovered Australia ... and you could include white kids in the school too so they would grow up with a positive attitude to Kooris'. Such a college – Koori Kollij – was established by Bruce McGuinness, a graduate of Monash and former Director of the VAAL, in 1984.

Fesl followed her interview in the *Herald* with a memorandum to the Vice Chancellor, Professor M. Logan, outlining her plans for the introduction of an Aboriginal Studies minor and major at Monash. Describing as 'mediocre' the presentation of Aboriginal Studies at other (unnamed) universities which 'failed to ... have the involvement of at least some Aboriginal lecturers', Fesl made it clear that Monash was well placed to 'lead Australia in the field of Aboriginal studies'. Not only did it have an existing core unit (Aboriginal Studies), but 'a potential workforce of tutors and lecturers' in Aboriginal students from the MOSA scheme. Eager to commence, and seeking to capitalise on the enthusiasm as well as discomfiture of the bicentenary, Fesl suggested that an announcement 'at the beginning of 1988' – or, better yet, timed to correspond with the Centre's move to its new home – would be particularly effective.

The ARC's long-standing accommodation worries ended with the move to new premises in 1988. Situated at Monash's front entrance, the multi-discipline center designed by Daryl Jackson, known as the Gallery Building, was formally opened by the State Minister for Aboriginal Affairs, Tom Roper, in May. Rather than announcing the introduction of an Aboriginal Studies minor and major, a development that would take another four years to be realised, Fesl used the occasion to publicise the Centre's newest initiative: a consultancy service in market research. In a creative bid to supplement its dwindling income, Fesl explained that the ARC would provide market research to Aboriginal people wishing to start new businesses. This followed the withdrawal of funding from the Department of Aboriginal Affairs, previously the Centre's main source of funding for operational costs. Cutbacks in government spending were felt across all areas as a result of the global stock market crash in 1987.

There was little time for seeking additional sources of funding during the bicentennial spree of activities and engagements. By 1989 the situation had deteriorated to such an extent that 'monetary matters [had] to be watched carefully'. Fesl complained that it was 'necessary for constant submission writing to be carried out if money [was] to be generated for Centre projects'. This was nothing new: what had changed was the need to include operational costs. In an increasingly crowded field, this made it difficult for the Centre to compete with other organisations and institutions such as the AIAS that were not similarly burdened. Two large projects tendered by the KRC in 1989 were awarded to the AIAS. Without an assured income to cover its operational costs, estimated at $30,000 per annum, the Centre was dependent on donations, money received for services rendered by the Director, and on the provision for administrative costs built into projects. The latter, as noted, had the effect of making the KRC non-competitive.

Fesl reported in April 1990 that the Centre's finances were in an 'unhealthy state'. With an operating balance of only $3903, it was clear that drastic action needed to be taken to keep the Centre alive. At the end of that year, despite reducing the staff to two, the Centre was more than $16,000 in deficit. Convinced that the Centre's ability to attract funding was dependent on the 'Director having and maintaining a high public profile', Fesl was 'often read in the press, seen on television or heard on the radio'. Increasingly asked to speak on the status of 'Koorie Women', she argued that what Koori women needed were role models: 'we need women to show the way, to visit and encourage others'. An important role model herself, to Fesl's long list of personal and professional achievements was added 'Victorian of the Year' in 1990. At one stage it was even suggested that she might be selected as Governor of Victoria!

By March 1991, the financial situation seemed brighter. A number of substantial private donations had been received, including $6000 from the Elizabeth Eggleston Trust, and $7500 from Norman Rothfield. The Victorian Education Department's decision to introduce Aboriginal Studies for Year 11 and 12 students presented several potentially lucrative opportunities for the KRC. In 1990 the Centre ran a special tutorial in its Aboriginal Studies program for Victorian Certificate of Education (VCE) teachers from Wesley College. The

College paid for the tutorial and associated administrative expenses. That year the KRC convened the inaugural meeting of the Hank Young Trust – Koorie Welfare and Education Reference Board (later the Hank Young Foundation for Aboriginal Welfare and Education). The aim of the Trust was to fund research and educational programs on a 'national basis for the Koorie community of Australia'. Extremely supportive of MOSA (see chapter 4), the Trust also provided generous financial assistance to the KRC. The KRC was invited to act as the Trust's secretariat during its initial year of operation; Fesl gladly accepted, noting that the Centre would, of course, 'be reimbursed for extra staff required to handle the workload and administration expenses incurred'. Following discussions with the Department of Education, the Hank Young Trust agreed to finance the development of a kit to aid in the teaching of Aboriginal Studies in schools. It was intended that the VCE kit be developed and marketed by the KRC as an income-generating venture. The first segment of the kit was trialed during 1992.

Although, at the end of 1992 the KRC's debit balance had increased to $36,858, Fesl expected that this would be 'fully covered' from the income from the sale of the VCE kits and a new project funded by Telecom on the 'needs of Koorie communities in remote areas'. Other creative sources of funding were sought. Negotiations with the newly established Aboriginal and Torres Strait Islander Commission resulted in a large grant of more than $200,000 being made to the Lordbja Victorian Language Centre which operated out of the KRC under Fesl's authority. The financial situation became even more complex following Monash University's merger with the Gippsland Institute of Advanced Education in 1989 which had its own Centre for Koori Studies (GCKS). During 1992 the Vice Chancellor and the

Professor Merle Ricklefs (left) and Professor Mal Logan
Source: Monash Archives

Academic Board agreed that a more unified management structure for Monash's Aboriginal programs was required. Appointed Head of Aboriginal Programs, Professor Merle Ricklefs produced a management structure designed to bring order and predictability, especially with regard to financial matters, to the KRC, MOSA and the GCKS. There was no suggestion of merging any of the programs.

Since 1988 the ARC/KRC and MOSA had been co-located in the Gallery Building, but they remained separate programs. Following the unexpected departure of MOSA's Director, John Austin, in March 1992, Fesl stepped 'into the breach', agreeing to act as Director of MOSA and the KRC in order 'to keep MOSA running' (see chapter 4). Finding MOSA in need of reform, Fesl instituted a number of staff changes that helped to improve administration and communication across the two programs. The Universities' internal auditor remarked that she seemed 'well in control of the situation' in May 1992. Although initially conceived as an 'unofficial amalgamation' and perceived by Fesl as beneficial to both units, her experience as head of the two programs led her to believe otherwise. After several months in the role she felt that to amalgamate would be to jeopardise the work of the KRC, for whereas the work of the KRC Director involved the 'need for long uninterrupted periods' of research and writing, the major part of the work of the Director of MOSA was 'interruptive' in nature. Fesl served in both capacities until April 1993.

Promoted to Associate Professor in January 1993, Fesl tendered her resignation as Director of the KRC in May, and left Monash in June to take up a position as Convener of Murrie Programs for the four campuses of Griffith University in Queensland. Serious questions were raised following her departure about the KRC's financial situation. Declining contributions from government and greatly reduced public donations coupled with irregularities in accounting meant that the KRC was now more than $50,000 in debt. The University decided to conduct a review of the KRC before a new Director was appointed. Carried out by Lachlan Chipman, Professor of Philosophy and Pro-vice Chancellor (Gippsland), the review took much longer to complete than expected. The position had still not been advertised when Acting Director of the KRC, Dr George Silberbauer, went on sabbatical in the first half of 1994. Meanwhile, the KRC's bewildered staff, uncertain about their future, 'withstood [the] assault on their morale' with courage and loyalty. It was the effect on students and the wider Aboriginal community that most worried Silberbauer. Concerned that their 'faith and interest in the

Centre' was dissipating, he called on the University to appoint a new Director without delay.

Sharon Firebrace: Committed to Community

A year and a half later, in mid 1995, Sharon Firebrace was appointed Director of the KRC. Descended from the Yorta Yorta people in eastern Victoria, Firebrace grew up in an orphanage in the 1960s. Like many Aboriginal people, she gained confidence through sport, representing Australia and Victoria in volleyball and netball. Firebrace attended the University of Melbourne, graduating with a Fine Arts degree; later she gained a Diploma of Education. Strongly community minded, she served as a senior executive with the VAAL for several years before establishing Palm River, an Aboriginal-focused public relations and cultural awareness training business, in the early 1990s. Her business achievements were recognised in her selection as the 1993–94 National and Victorian Indigenous Businesswoman of the Year. In 1995 Palm River was contracted by the Department of the Prime Minister and Cabinet to work on the national Reconciliation project. Firebrace, who commenced work at Monash in May that year, negotiated a less than full-time load as KRC Director in order to accommodate her extensive business and community interests.

Conscious of the extent to which the Centre's work had stalled, during her first month in the job Firebrace produced a register of proposed new projects for the KRC. These included: the establishment of an Aboriginal language laboratory which, building upon the KRC's earlier Bundjalung program, would develop Aboriginal languages suitable for primary and secondary school curricula; an anthology of Aboriginal literature that could be employed in Aboriginal studies programs in universities; and a library supplementation program to enhance the scope of available reference material in the Elizabeth Eggleston library. Further brainstorming produced a list of potential research topics and supplementary questions, including: Aboriginal Women and the Law ('how responsive is the law to Aboriginal women's needs?'); Aboriginal Women and Feminism ('what is more important – race or gender?'); The Dialectic of Aboriginality ('what does Aboriginality entail for Aborigines?'); ATSIC ('what do Aboriginal people think of ATSIC?'); Survival of the Kinship System in Urban Settings ('to what extent has it survived?'). A program of possible new courses, based on suggestions from KRC students and staff, was also compiled. These included: Women's Role and Status in Aboriginal Society; Aborigines in Sport/ the Mass Media / Art; and Aboriginal Literature.

Reflecting a burgeoning interest in the status of Aboriginal women and other contemporary issues, Firebrace's proposed research topics and courses demonstrated her engagement with the world of academia. The larger projects represented her attempt to engage with the findings of various reviews into Aboriginal and Torres Strait Islander education which had highlighted the need for greater inclusion of Indigenous Studies in mainstream education, as well as the findings of the Royal Commission into Aboriginal Death in Custody (RCADIC) which stressed the importance of valuing and maintaining Aboriginal culture. Although not all of her ideas were taken up, several new subjects, including Aborigines and Women, were introduced during her directorship that proved successful in attracting both indigenous and non-indigenous students to the KRC. A measure of the impact of the report of the RCADIC, the University now considered Koori Studies subjects to be 'exercises in reconciliation, as well as awareness raising strategies'.

MAKING A DIFFERENCE

Firebrace visited several Asian countries in 1995 and made contacts at universities in Japan, Thailand and Hong-Kong. The following year, as a guest of the American government through the International Visitors Program, she visited the United States. During the course of the visit, she gave interviews comparing the socio-political circumstances of Australia's Indigenous people with Indigenous Americans of the Navajo Nation, and African-Americans. Soon after her return, the KRC launched a series of three discussion papers on Aboriginal peoples' contact with the Victorian criminal justice, education, and health systems. The initial paper, written by KRC research fellow Michael Mackay, comprised the first comprehensive survey of Aboriginal arrests in Victoria since the 1991 RCADIC. Showing a sharp rise in the rate of police processing of Aboriginal youth between 1993–95, it attracted considerable media attention.

Heavily involved in the reconciliation process, Firebrace resigned as Director of the KRC in February 1997 to devote more time to community and business activities. Under her directorship, the Centre had begun to regain some of its lost energy and focus, but it was a long way from reclaiming its preeminent position as a leading research facility. Her resignation coincided with the commencement of a review of Monash's Aboriginal programs conducted by Professor Colin Bourke and Associate Professor Eleanor Bourke from the University of South Australia. Given a broad brief from the Vice Chancellor, David Robinson, the Bourkes' were tasked with investigating the strengths and weaknesses of MOSA, the KRC and the GCKS. Their report, completed towards the end of 1997, heralded the beginning of a new regime that is described in chapter five.

Conclusion

Over the two decades reviewed here, the employment and training of young Aboriginal people stands out as one of the CRAA/ARC/KRC's main achievements. In providing opportunities for young Aboriginal people to learn skills and develop confidence in their interactions with the white world, the Centre played an important role in the growth of a new generation of Aboriginal community leaders. At the same time, in conducting research of direct relevance to Aboriginal people by Aboriginal people, it helped to promote agency and ownership of Aboriginal studies. It also helped to change wider community attitudes, generating deeper understandings of Aboriginal people, Aboriginal culture and the effects of discrimination. Set against the constant battle to gain funding from the University and federal bureaucracy, the need to seek private donors just to stay alive, the need to convince the University of the academic merit of its courses, and divisions within the Aboriginal community, these achievements appear all the more remarkable. Although, by the end of the 1990s the University was becoming more supportive of Koori research and the teaching of Koori studies, seeing these as part of its contribution to reconciliation, for most of its history the Centre faced challenges not experienced by other academic units. These challenges called for an exceptionally high level of leadership capability, as well as personal charisma and charm, which each Director had, but which, over time and under extreme pressure, inevitably wore down, contributing to the difficulties experienced by Fesl, the Centre's longest serving Director to that point. Viewed in this light, keeping the Centre going in the face of multiple extreme pressures must also stand as a significant achievement.

Chapter 4

MOSA: CREATING OPPORTUNITIES

In 1980 only 0.3 percent of Aboriginal school leavers commenced tertiary education in comparison to more than 2 percent of non-Aboriginal school leavers, and many failed to complete. In 1983 fewer than 800 Aboriginal people were enrolled in higher education courses around the country. At Monash University, only two Aboriginal people were enrolled that year, one of whom was Eve Fesl. From 1984, when the Monash Orientation Scheme for Aborigines (MOSA) commenced, to 1998 when it was disbanded due to falling enrolments, more than 200 Aboriginal students gained a certificate equivalent to matriculation and an introduction to university life which saw a credible portion pursue higher education at Monash or elsewhere.

The story of MOSA is another story of talented and dedicated individuals working beyond their remit to make a difference for Aboriginal people at Monash. The brainchild of Colin Bourke, Merle Ricklefs and Eve Fesl, MOSA came into existence at the beginning of a wave of change in the provision of education for Aboriginal people. In backing MOSA, Monash established a model and a precedent for Aboriginal enrolment in university that exposed inequalities and transformed educational pathways for Aboriginal people. In November 1985, at the end of MOSA's second year, a House of Representatives Select Committee report on Aboriginal Education called on universities to 'develop bridging courses and enclaves for Aboriginal studies to enable them to gain entry to a wide range of university courses'. The Committee noted that Monash was the only university to provide such a course: whereas 'many tertiary institutions have been prepared to modify their entry requirements', 'Monash stands alone' in attempting to bridge the 'educational and cultural gap'. By the end of the following decade, there were pathway schemes in operation at universities throughout the nation. Focusing on the leadership provided by Ricklefs and others in establishing and running MOSA, this chapter documents the program's rise and fall in the context of wider educational reform and changing educational priorities for Aboriginal people.

'What You Need is a Bridging Course'

Building on Colin Bourke's parting advice that what was needed at Monash was a bridging or pre-university year for Aboriginal students, Merle Ricklefs, Professor of History, involved Eve Fesl, Director of the Aboriginal Research Centre, David Bradley, Professor of English, and W.H. Scott, Professor of Sociology, in working out the details of a comprehensive 'proposal for a special program to overcome the educational disadvantages of Aboriginal students at tertiary level'. American-born Ricklefs had been active in the civil rights movement in the United States during the 1960s and had worked in London during the racially-tense Enoch Powell era. His sensitivity to racial issues was heightened and, just as importantly, not having grown up in Australia, he 'didn't know that it [increasing Aboriginal enrolments at university] couldn't be done'.

MOSA students
Source: Monash Archives

In May 1981 Ricklefs drew up a discussion paper that identified the main aim of the scheme as being 'to improve mature Aboriginal students' prospects of completing undergraduate degrees so as to increase, in particular, the number of Aboriginal teachers and lawyers in the community'. The paper, at this stage just a statement of general ideas, rested on the assumption that 'autonomous Aboriginal advancement is a desired aim and that Aboriginal schoolteachers and lawyers must eventually play a role in such advancement'. Displaying his characteristic optimism, Ricklefs expected that the preliminary year would, 'in due course, render itself unnecessary' through achieving an 'end [to] the 'second-class' status of Aboriginals in the educational world'.

A key feature of the proposed scheme was that 'upon satisfactory completion ... of the preliminary year, students should be guaranteed admission into the Monash Faculties of Education, Law, and Arts'. This aspect of the discussion paper, which was circulated to interested parties throughout the University and outside it, attracted the most comment. University registrar, J.D. Butchart was 'most unhappy' about guaranteeing Aborigines 'a place on a non-competitive basis'; he viewed it as 'discriminatory'. From the beginning Monash had been required by statute to maintain the same academic standards as the University of Melbourne, a requirement that Butchart was keen to preserve. Although he advised Ricklefs that he 'would not mind at all if *your Aborigines* who complete the preliminary year are then said to have been ranked as best we can and selected on merit', his condescending tone suggested otherwise. Ricklefs met Butchart's objection easily: 'There is no question of guaranteeing places in advance', he explained. Instead, the 'pre-tertiary year would finish with a competitive examination, and places would be offered only to candidates who had performed satisfactorily on that examination'. Pressure to regard the preliminary year as preparation for the Australian Scholastic Aptitude Test came from several quarters, but Ricklefs resisted all attempts to subject Aboriginal students to additional examination. Rather than exercising positive discrimination, Ricklefs argued that the 'principle behind the whole proposal [was] not, of course, to give a special advantage to anyone, but rather to ameliorate the special disadvantage suffered by Aboriginals in the education field'.

By the end of 1981 Ricklefs and his co-planners had drafted a second proposal. This version, a ten-page typescript document covering everything from student numbers and admission procedures, to staffing and the university community, was submitted to the Deans of Arts and Law, to the ARC, and to the Vice Chancellor for general endorsement. Further revisions were made and plans established for the next phase. A clear separation of tasks was established: while Ricklefs continued to cajole the University, Fesl did the same with Aboriginal organisations and committees.

Fesl was responsible for placing the revised proposal on the agenda of the National Aboriginal Education Committee (NAEC) meeting in February 1982. The NAEC's agenda revolved around the training of Aboriginal teachers. It saw the bridging scheme as a way of achieving its goal of 1000 qualified Aboriginal teachers by the end of the decade, and so was supportive. However, rather than limit the program to Monash, the NAEC 'considered that Monash University should be deleted from the proposal and the proposal should be written so as to apply to all universities'. Although the Dean of the Faculty of Law, Professor R. Baxt, made a similar suggestion – namely, that consideration be given to 'cooperation with other institutions in the mounting of such a program' – this suggestion was not taken up.

Nevertheless the NAEC's support was crucial. A body comprised wholly of Aboriginal members, its desire to see the scheme implemented in other universities was transformed by Ricklefs into a statement on the proposal's intrinsic value: the NAEC 'regards [the] proposal as being a model of what ought to be done by Universities', he exclaimed. The NAEC's support enabled Ricklefs to defend the proposal as not only Aboriginal-*inspired*, but Aboriginal-*authorised*. At every opportunity he stressed that Colin Bourke had first proposed the scheme, and that in pursing the proposal he was responding to what the Aboriginal community said it wanted: 'We are trying to respond to legitimate requests from Aboriginal people for special university programs to solve their special problems'. For similar reasons, he emphasised Fesl's membership of the 'core planning group' and direct involvement 'in every step of the planning', and that the ARC Board – 'a majority of whose members are Aboriginal' – and the Victorian Aboriginal Education Consultative Group had approved the proposal. These statements were all true, but Ricklefs' own role was also crucial. He drove the process, answering criticisms, finding solutions and providing leadership at every juncture.

Conscious that similar programs were already in operation elsewhere, and anxious not to duplicate services, Ricklefs approached the coordinators of bridging courses for Aboriginal students at the South Australian and Western Australian Institutes of Technology (SAIT and WAIT); later he and Fesl visited SAIT and WAIT to learn as much as possible about their experiences. Ricklefs also got in touch with authorities at the University of New South Wales where a special entry scheme for Aboriginal applicants lacking normal matriculation qualifications was in existence. His enquiries left him convinced that what he was proposing for Monash was 'unique among universities' in Australia. Indeed, this was part of its appeal. Ricklefs recognised the leading role Monash had already played in establishing the Aboriginal Research Centre and sought to build upon this, claiming that:

> The Orientation Year program will allow Monash to exercise further educational and moral leadership within the wider community, and to demonstrate that this University not only recognizes and analyses contemporary issues, but also has the imagination and commitment to contribute to their resolution.

By May 1982 the proposal had received the backing of the Arts and Law Faculty Boards, and the Board of the ARC, but there was still considerable opposition. With the proposal scheduled to go before the Professorial Board at the end of June, Ricklefs spent most of that month lobbying for support.

Even those in favour of the scheme, such as Professor W.A. Rachinger (Department of Physics) found much to criticise. Anticipating the concerns of others, Rachinger questioned whether the proposed orientation year would be better placed in a secondary institution, and whether it would debase the existing matriculation criteria. Fine-tuned through repetition, Ricklefs' response cut to the core of the issue: 'only a university can do what we propose', he replied, because only a university has the necessary 'prestige'. Monash's reputation as a top university was important in terms of attracting both 'the most promising students' and financial support. But there was also another factor: 'only by preparing students at the same institution where they will then carry on as tertiary students can one achieve the continuity which is thought to be important in the success achieved by similar programs at WAIT and SAIT.' Moreover, hosting the scheme would enable Monash to 'keep direct control' of its own admissions.

Addressing the issue at the heart of nearly all concerns about the scheme, Ricklefs explained that it would not lower matriculation standards. Quite the contrary, it would raise the skills of Aboriginal students to Monash's matriculation requirements. Importantly, he pointed out that this was different to what was being at other Australian universities (including the University of Melbourne) that had 'waived all matriculation criteria for Aboriginal people', requiring merely an interview. It was also different from what was being done in the United States where some universities had created courses within their degree structures that were below university standard as a means of 'accelerating the entrance of disadvantaged citizens into tertiary study'. Viewed in this comparative light, Ricklefs noted that his proposal was 'in fact a conservative measure'.

To Ricklefs great surprise and delight, the Professorial Board 'overwhelmingly approved' the proposal for an orientation year for intending Aboriginal undergraduate students at Monash University at its meeting on 30 June 1982. With the University firmly behind the scheme, it went to Council for final endorsement on 12 July and was approved pending finance. 'It was an exciting time at Monash', Ricklefs later recalled. The scheme's most strident critics now fell in behind him determined to make it 'the best program of its kind'. In a press release announcing the scheme, Ricklefs highlighted its 'bridging' and 'enclave' elements. The former, he explained, sought to 'bridge the educational, psychological, and cultural gap' which existed between Aboriginal and other first year university students, while the latter aimed to provide a specific locale and staff which would act as a support mechanism for Aboriginal students. Monash had shown 'national leadership' in encouraging the plan, but whether it went any further depended on government providing the necessary funding.

The Professorial Board established a committee to consider the implementation of the scheme which, subject to finance, was due to commence in 1984: Ricklefts (Chairman), Fesl, Professors R. Baxt, J.D. Legge and J.M. Swan were appointed. Professor Graeme Davison (History Department) was appointed later as Deputy Chairman. The committee's first task was to decide on a name for the scheme. Ricklefs wanted an 'elegant name' with a memorable acronym: he liked OPEN (Orientation Program and Entry), but it failed to produce much enthusiasm. The preferred option was MOSA (Monash Orientation Scheme for Aborigines). The committee sought to resolve questions of accommodation and staffing, but it was funding that dominated much of their work. Without funds, all other matters were moot. A prospectus was prepared and distributed to relevant Commonwealth Departments in September 1982. In principle agreements were reached for a joint funding arrangement between the Departments of Education and Aboriginal Affairs, but no formal offers could be made until after the Federal Budget was handed down in the middle of the following year. This created a potential stumbling block, for without guaranteed funding, the committee could not advertise for staff or students. In 'the absence of any negative advice … and in the light of the pressing time considerations', the committee's solution was to proceed with conditional advertisements for the positions of director and teacher. Advertisements were also placed for students. In September 1983, just months before the first intake of students was due to arrive, funding sufficient to cover staffing and administrative costs was secured. MOSA was 'in business'.

The planning and negotiating that resulted in MOSA's establishment took place in a wider context of changing approaches to Aboriginal education. In 1982 Tranby Aboriginal College in Sydney established an Aboriginal Education Preparatory course that, like MOSA, sought to ease the transition for people who were returning to study as adults. Koori Kollij, established in Melbourne in 1984, also sought to rectify the deficiencies in Aboriginal peoples' primary and secondary schooling by offering courses in 'black studies' in an environment that was supportive of students' Aboriginal identity.

In Adelaide, the Aboriginal Community College helped students develop skills they could use in obtaining employment. The growth of these autonomous Aboriginal colleges demonstrated a felt need within the Aboriginal community for adult education programs that was not being met elsewhere.

The Commonwealth and state governments were listening, but change was slow in coming. By the mid 1980s, it was increasingly accepted that 'Aboriginal people [were] best equipped to define their own educational needs and that, to the greatest extent possible, Aboriginal people should be involved in establishing the aims and objectives of Aboriginal polices and programs'. Embracing this principle, MOSA's planning group decided that, if at all possible, the Director of the program 'should ... be of Aboriginal origin'. The desirability of this was debated by the Committee for Undergraduate Studies in the Faculty of Arts which, although divided, eventually agreed that the appointment should be 'the best available, irrespective of racial origin'. Indicative of the poor state of cultural awareness then current at Monash, the Committee for Undergraduate Studies further agreed that 'if no Aboriginal were suitable, an American black or an American Indian might represent an appropriate alternative'. No one was expecting Isaac Brown.

Isaac Brown

The 'key to MOSA's success' during its early years was its first Director, Isaac Brown. Fesl's reaction, vividly recalled by Ricklefs, summed up the selection panel's amazement when Brown was interviewed: 'who is he, where did he come from?' 'Softly spoken, engaging, gentle, and with an accent that sounded like it was the product of the English public school system', Brown made a lasting impression. Born in Darwin, Brown's Indigenous ancestors were Iwaidja and Torres Strait Islander peoples. He attended school in Alice Springs and Darwin, Teachers College in Adelaide, the Australian College of Speech Therapists in Melbourne, and gained a Bachelor of Applied Science from the Victoria Institute of Colleges. Before coming to Monash, he worked as a teacher, speech pathologist, and Director of Clinical Education in the School of Communication Disorders at the Lincoln Institute of Health Sciences. At the time of his appointment as Director of MOSA, he was working with the Victorian Health Commission.

Brown selected Dr Janice Newton, a Monash graduate with a Diploma of Education and a PhD in Anthropology, to teach alongside him in MOSA's foundation year. Aided by Juanita Page, Brown's very capable secretary, and the MOSA Committee, chaired by Ricklefs, Brown and Newton began recruiting students at the end of 1983. Based on advice from the conveners of the bridging courses at SAIT and WAIT, it was decided that the students should all be mature, aged twenty-one or over, and should be selected from around Australia. The SAIT program, known as the Aboriginal Task Force, had had the most success with students who came from further away and were therefore detached from family demands; Ricklefs, keen to give the first cohort every chance of success, kept this in mind in the selection of students for MOSA. Both he and Brown felt it was important, especially in the first year, to choose candidates with 'stickability'. Potential students were asked to write two-hundred words on why they wished to study at university, what sort of career they hoped a university degree might lead to, and how well qualified they felt they were to enter the MOSA scheme.

MOSA: CREATING OPPORTUNITIES

Isaac Brown
Source: Monash Archives
Photographer: Richard Crompton

The most suitable candidates were invited to Monash to see the campus and meet the staff. Newton recalled the importance of this (all expenses paid) introduction to university life: 'we gave them a lecture, then we sent them to the library to answer comprehensive questions – in quiet with no smoking … and then, after that, if they were still wanting to do it' they knew what they were signing up for.

'A lot of people self-selected out', Newton said, when they realised how 'how boringly awful' university life could be. Final decisions were made at the conclusion of this two-way evaluation. MOSA's selection procedures ensured that all students granted admission were of a certain academic calibre and that their motivation was high; anything less would have been setting people up for failure.

Twenty applications were received from all the mainland states and the Northern Territory, and nine students were selected for MOSA's foundation year. Of these seven started in February 1984, and six completed the year: Brian McNamee, Barbara Nona, Fiona Hill, Gary Martin, Janette Bibby and Gwenda Davis. All six achieved a standard at least equal to the Higher School Certificate, qualifying them to proceed to first year undergraduate study in Arts or Law. Bibby and Nona were the first MOSA students to graduate, gaining Arts degrees in 1988. Martin completed his Arts degree in 1990.

Most MOSA students had completed at least Year 10 at high school, although some had a much lower standard of education. Preparing them for university meant helping them to develop general study and communication skills, read and make notes accurately, follow lectures, use a library, define and develop essay topics, write effectively, contribute orally to seminar and tutorial discussions, and sit examinations. These objectives were achieved within a course structure that approximated first year university work, but was based on HSC course descriptions. With only two teachers and limited resources, Brown and Newton worked out a year-long program which included core subjects in numeracy and communication skills, as well as three discipline areas: English, History, and Anthropology and Sociology. Contact hours were twelve per week, leaving plenty of time for private study.

MOSA: CREATING OPPORTUNITIES

Director of MOSA, Isaac Brown, with Gary Martin and his daughter
Source: Monash Archives
Photographer: Richard Crompton

MOSA was committed to achieving 'success by cultural reinforcement'; that is, by 'encouraging pride … in Aboriginal culture' and Aboriginal identity. In practice, this meant including Aboriginal people, culture and history as topic areas, and setting readings by Aboriginal authors, poets and playwrights. Colin Bourke, Colin Johnson and Isobel Whites' book, *Before the Invasion: Aboriginal*

Life to 1788, was set as preliminary reading in all three discipline areas in 1986. Newton recalled that at least 60 percent of the content of the three discipline areas was Aboriginal. 'Getting the students to feel proud of their history ... and culture' was not only 'empowering', she reflected, it also helped them to stay focused and interested in learning. Certainly this was Kerrie Keleher's experience. She became aware of her Indigenous heritage in the late 1980s and enrolled in MOSA in 1993. Learning about Indigenous history really 'fired [her] up': 'it changed my life', she recalled, 'because I didn't have any of that growing up'.

Another way MOSA sought to encourage racial pride was with reference to other minority groups. Newton, who taught History and Anthropology/Sociology, included lectures on the contact history of Native Americans, racial attitudes to the Chinese in Australia during the gold-rush, the migrant experience in Australia, and race relations in South Africa. She received help from a range of people in the History Department (in whose corridor on the 6th floor of the Menzies Building MOSA was located), including Daniel Potts, Graeme Davison, Marian Quartly, and Andrew Markus.

Given all the pressures that MOSA students faced, Ricklefs was determined that they should not have to work in addition to their studies. Most students received a stipend from the Aboriginal Study Grants Scheme (ABSTUDY) – $70.75 per week, with a dependent's allowance of $42.70 plus $10 for each additional dependent. This being insufficient to live on, Ricklefs established a 'welfare fund' based on private donations to be used primarily as a means of subsidising living costs, and as a source of emergency support in times of crisis. His goal was $10,000 for the foundation year and he reached this before the end of 1983 with major donations from the Elizabeth

Eggleston Fund, the Herbert Vere Evatt Memorial Foundation, the William Buckland Foundation, the Lance Reichstein Charitable Foundation, and the Helen M. Schutt Trust. Students were asked to estimate housing, travel, child-care and establishment costs, and were paid from the welfare fund on a monthly basis. They could also apply for special loans to cover unforeseen expenses such as car repairs, medical costs and court fines.

One of MOSA's most distinctive and important features, the welfare fund was an important contributor to the program's success, but it was not without its problems. Uneasy about his role in the allocation of funds, Brown stated soon after his appointment that he preferred 'not to be involved'. It was not that he disapproved of the scheme, it was more that he wished to separate teaching from money distribution. Elizabeth Nelson (later Reed), appointed a MOSA teacher in 1987, found the welfare fund extremely problematic: 'not in the sense that it helped students … but [in it] being called a welfare fund'. She 'found it excruciatingly difficult talking about the welfare fund' because she 'felt like [she] was a mission lady'. Probably Brown felt the same way. His reservations notwithstanding, managing the welfare fund was part of the Director's job and Brown handled it with 'care and precision'.

MOSA experienced steady growth during its first three years; the number of students increased to twelve (ten completions) in 1985, and fifteen (eleven completions) in 1986. An additional part-time teacher, Dr Angela Risdale, was employed to teach English in 1985, and guaranteed admission to qualified MOSA graduates was granted by the Faculty of Economics and Politics (ECOPS). The achievement of the latter tested Ricklefs redoubtable skills in diplomacy. Numerous carefully worded memorandums addressed to

Professor W.A. Sinclair, Dean of ECOPS, left his office between July and October that year. Ricklefs carefully explained the process by which MOSA students were recommended for admission to Arts and/or Law by the MOSA Committee on the basis of advice from the MOSA Board of Examiners. Before agreeing to accept MOSA students, Sinclair required a 'firm understanding that the MOSA Committee would not go against the advice of the representative of the Faculty [of ECOPS] on the Committee with respect to whether a satisfactory standard had been achieved by the applicant'. His patience pushed to the limit, Ricklefs assured Sinclair that while he 'would have the power to reject a MOSA candidate', MOSA's assessment structures were intended to ensure that 'we would never put you into a position in which you would feel obliged to do so'.

Like its recruitment process, MOSA's assessment structures were extremely rigorous. The minutes of the fortnightly meetings attended by MOSA staff serve as a record of the high level of academic monitoring, as well as professional and personal care and attention, each student received throughout the year. The meetings held in May and September 1986 were typical. Each student's progress was discussed, examination results scrutinised, and individualised programs for improvement worked out. Students who were struggling were offered extra tutorials, while students who were doing well were set 'further readings ... to extend [their] ability'. Non-attendance at tutorials was noted and remedial action planned. In cases where students appeared depressed or in need of extra attention, Brown or one of the other teachers was assigned to provide moral support. Even with this close degree of supervision, not everyone passed the MOSA year. Of the eleven students who completed the MOSA program in 1986, two failed, and nine were recommended by the MOSA Board of Examiners for admission to Monash University. Of these, one was considered admissible to ECOPS, but chose to enroll in Arts instead.

Not every student recommended for admission ended up studying at Monash, or completing degrees; some chose to attend different universities; some returned to their jobs with the prospect of promotion; some withdrew from university study, often for family related reasons, only to send their children (sometimes referred to as 'MOSA babies') in later years. From the outset it was understood that 'success' needed to be considered broadly. However, for the purpose of securing funding, 'success' in the narrow sense of increasing the number of Aboriginal people with tertiary qualifications was what mattered, and MOSA looked set to achieve this. In 1987 there were thirty-four Aboriginal students on campus: thirteen in the orientation year, eleven undergraduates in Arts, eight in Arts/Law, one in Economics/Law, and one in Economics.

In 1984–86, funding sufficient to cover MOSA's staffing costs was received from the Department of Aboriginal Affairs, and the Department of Education on an annual basis, while Monash provided accommodation and facilities. At the end of 1986, this funding pattern gave rise 'to a crisis so severe that the very survival of the programme ... was called into question'. Without warning, the Department of Education reduced its annual grant by more than $13,000, being the cost of the employer's contribution for the Director's superannuation. Ricklefs' impassioned telex message to Prime Minister Robert (Bob) Hawke captured the urgency of the situation. Frustrated, Ricklefs explained that the Department of Education had undertaken 'unequivocally to meet these costs' when the original funding agreement was reached, but now refused. He fumed:

> APPARENTLY FOR THIS BUREAUCRATIC REASON THE ONLY BRIDGING AND ENCLAVE SCHEME FOR ABORIGINES IN AN AUSTRALIAN UNIVERSITY – A SCHEME WITH MUCH SUCCESS BEHIND IT AND GREAT PROMISE AHEAD – MAY BE SHUT DOWN.
>
> MORE SUSPICIOUS MINDS SUGGEST THAT THERE IS A DELIBERATE POLICY TO STOP MOSA BECAUSE OF ITS VERY SUCCESS, FOR THE EMERGENCE OF A MORE HIGHLY EDUCATED ABORIGINAL LEADERSHIP MAY THREATEN VESTED INTERESTS IN BOTH THE WHITE AND ABORIGINAL COMMUNITIES.
>
> BUT WE ARE PLAYING FOR LARGER STAKES. WE ARE PLAYING FOR DIGNITY, FOR PROGRESS, FOR UNDERSTANDING AND FOR JUSTICE. I BEG YOU TO INTERVENE PERSONALLY TO SAVE MOSA.

Ricklefs was convinced that the shortfall 'would be the end of MOSA': 'it will be necessary for us to terminate one of the teaching positions, with the effect that serious questions must arise as to the viability of the entire MOSA teaching program'. There were no sinister motives; the Department of Education simply sought a greater contribution from Monash. After weeks of 'lobbying and politicking, telexing, and telephoning Canberra', the full level of funding was restored.

During 1987 the Commonwealth Tertiary Education Commission (CTEC) began urging universities to enroll Aboriginal students in what it called 'professional faculties', especially law, medicine, and engineering. Given that the Law Faculty at Monash was already involved in MOSA, Monash's Vice Chancellor, Ray Martin, encouraged Ricklefs and Brown to think of ways of expanding MOSA to include laboratory-based disciplines. Initial discussions with the Deans of the Faculties of Medicine,

Engineering, and Science proved positive. It was agreed that the 'preparation of unqualified Aboriginal candidates for laboratory-based faculties would ... require an extension of [MOSA] into a two-year program'. Ricklefs prepared a proposal for the CTEC outlining the costs, and requesting a commitment of an additional $50,000 per annum for at least three to five years. It quickly became apparent, however, that CTEC's priority was to fund 'special places' for Aboriginal undergraduates, not university preparation courses. Ricklefs riposte revealed his growing level of irritation with the short-sightedness of government policy: 'special places' that were not accompanied by 'special preparation and support facilities' meant laying 'the grounds for failure'.

In a lengthy document on 'The Future of MOSA' prepared in May 1987 at the request of the Vice Chancellor, Ricklefs laid out his recommendations for the expansion of MOSA. His plan hinged on Monash recognising MOSA as 'successful, academically respectable, good for Monash, good for Aboriginal people, and good for the Australian society as whole'. Expanding on these points, Ricklefs observed:

> MOSA has given Monash a national role in a very important area of educational development. MOSA also plays a role in an important social change within Australia, for I believe that we will soon see the emergence of a highly educated Aboriginal group, which will influence not only the future of the Aboriginal people of Australia, but also that of Australian society as a whole.

If Monash accepted that MOSA was all these things, if it wished MOSA to continue and was 'interested in experimenting with an extension into laboratory-based faculties', then Ricklefs' recommendation was for the University to agree to fund the Director's position for a fixed-term period of five years, freeing up other sources of funding for additional teachers salaries and other expenses associated with the development of a science-stream.

While Monash considered its options, Dr Deirdre Jordan from the University of Adelaide was engaged to conduct an independent external review of MOSA's effectiveness, its success and failure rates, management structures, and teaching and funding arrangements. Overall, Jordan found MOSA to be 'highly effective'. Her only substantive criticism was leveled at government for failing to provide MOSA with ongoing financial support. She called on the CTEC to recognise MOSA as 'a program of national significance which may be used as a model for other programs which provide access to University education not only for Aboriginal people, but for the disadvantaged in general', and to take responsibility for funding MOSA in its entirety on a triennial basis. Jordan gave the proposal to broaden the options available to Aboriginal students to include laboratory-based faculties her 'strongest support'.

CTEC could not be persuaded to take over the funding of MOSA. Instead, in keeping with Ricklefs' proposal, Monash agreed to commit itself to bearing the cost of Brown's position for five years. An accord was reached with the newly created Department of Employment, Education and Training (DEET) at the end of 1987 enabling current funding provided by the Department of Education to be redirected towards the cost of two new staff appointments in the science area. The Department of Aboriginal Affairs Education and Training Programs was transferred to DEET at the same time, effectively creating a single funding body for MOSA.

The science stream commenced with an enrollment of six students in 1988. MOSA's first two science teachers, Felicia Birman and Phil

Heraud, developed a rigorous course in mathematics, physics and chemistry which included sixteen to twenty contact hours per week, of which four to six hours were spent in the laboratory. Rob Hyatt was among the first intake of students in the science stream. Unlike his fellow students, most of whom had had no previous science education or higher mathematical training, Hyatt had studied science in Year 11 and 12. Having failed to pass, Brown had made a special case for his acceptance into MOSA (see below) and he proved to be an excellent student. This was only partly a reflection of his previous experience and background knowledge. Hyatt reflected that he 'found it easy because of the environment' created by the teachers and the other students: 'we were all together as the MOSA family'. For Hyatt, whose sense of Aboriginal identity was not very strong when he commenced the program, the mentoring he received from his fellow students was as important, perhaps even more so, than the formal learning: 'the academic side led me on a path of work … but in terms of my Aboriginality … I don't know where I'd be without that', he explained. After completing the two-year MOSA science course, Hyatt enrolled in a Science degree, graduating with honours in 1994. He completed a Masters at RMIT in 1998 and later accepted a position with the Victorian State Government. Now state coordinator of the Aboriginal Sport Recreation program, he says his life was transformed by MOSA and the knowledge gained about 'what it is to be Aboriginal'.

The launch of the science stream coincided with MOSA's move to the Gallery Building where it was rehoused alongside the Aboriginal Research Centre. Although symbolically significant in the sense that Monash's Aboriginal programs were now co-located at the 'front door to the University' and in its 'most prestigious building',

Isaac Brown (second from right) and Minister for Aboriginal Affairs Gerry Hand (second from left) talking with students on the balcony of the Gallery Building at Monash
Source: Monash Archives
Photographer: Richard Crompton

the move away from the 6th floor of the Menzies building had the effect of isolating MOSA students from the mainstream. Not that this bothered Hyatt. While studying for his science degree, Hyatt 'spent every day at MOSA', utilising the enclave space provided in the Gallery Building. As a MOSA graduate he continued to receive tutoring, and was supported by the welfare fund, but it was the 'family' side of things that drew him back. This was MOSA's 'parallel function'. Its primary function was academic, to assist 'Aboriginal people throughout Australia to gain access to tertiary education'; at the same time it aimed 'to provide personal support and encouragement to Aboriginal students to help them gain the confidence and sense of self-esteem necessary to enable them to compete in the large and demanding world of the University'.

MOSA: CREATING OPPORTUNITIES

Brown took the pastoral care side of his responsibilities very seriously. He helped the students find housing, manage their money, and dress appropriately – sometimes all at the same time: Ricklefs remembered Brown saying to students from the Northern Territory who were walking around Monash in thongs, shorts and t-shirts, 'this is the winter time … [let's] buy you some coats, some warmer clothes and then you won't need to heat the house to 28 degrees'. A master at cultural negotiation, Brown trained one student from a remote community how to pay, rather than barter, for goods. Nothing was too much trouble: he oversaw a smoking ceremony at the house of a student who felt it contained a malign presence; he took a group of students to the snow who had never experienced it before; he 'would visit students at midnight if he had to, if something went wrong'; he invited students to his house for meals; and regularly ate dinner at the Monash Halls of Residence in order to provide the Aboriginal students domiciled there with additional support. Students needing extra care were sometimes taken fishing on weekends, the peace and tranquility providing an opportunity for one-on-one mentoring and advice. Being Aboriginal, knowing the circumstances that many of the students came from, understanding the 'lack of confidence' that stemmed from being an outsider 'in that big space' at Monash, Brown could relate on many levels. His very presence at MOSA encouraged students to challenge themselves. Helen Curzon-Siggers (later Bnads) explained that Brown 'unleashed … the joyfulness of being in that big place' by creating a safe space to come back to at MOSA.

When Hyatt, underage and unsure of his Aboriginal heritage, presented for an interview with Brown in 1987 having just failed Year 12, he was more than nervous: 'I was really scared, you know, I'm fairly fair'. Correctly interpreting the source of Hyatt's apprehension, Brown handed him a poem, 'Kooris come in all colours' (by Carol Kendall) which immediately put him at his ease. Despite being only eighteen years old, Brown supported Hyatt's admission to the MOSA program. Flexibility with regard to admissions was an important feature of the MOSA program. The majority of students were aged over twenty-one, but exceptions were made on a case-by-case basis. In Hyatt's case, Brown argued that because he was intending to study science, and because MOSA's science-stream – which was due to commence that year – took two years to complete, Hyatt would be twenty years old, and therefore a 'mature' student, by the time he reached undergraduate studies. It was a winning argument!

Brown's commitment to student welfare, and level of involvement in their lives, was matched by many of the staff at MOSA. Newton attended social gatherings (housewarmings and 'Mary Kay' make-up parties) at students' houses, and accompanied one student to the ballet to see Giselle. Reed recalled attending NADOC rallies with MOSA students, but it was Angela Risdale who really went the extra mile. Unmarried, Christian and aged in her late fifties, Risdale saw MOSA as a kind of calling: 'it seemed to me like a life direction', she recalled. Wanting to 'make a difference' in her students' lives, Risdale helped them to set up their rented homes, providing linen from her own cupboards, tea-sets, cooking equipment, crockery and furniture. Many students developed 'strong personal relationships' with her that helped them in times of crisis. The result, as documented in the Jordan review, was that students 'learned to establish coping mechanisms so that, while always suffering from a lack of financial [security], for most of them this [was] not allowed to reach proportions of a magnitude which would prevent their continuation with the course'.

MOSA: CREATING OPPORTUNITIES

Isaac Brown with MOSA students
Source: Monash Archives
Photographer: Richard Crompton

Ricklefs and Brown were never sure from one year to the next whether the generosity of the welfare fund's donors (mostly private foundations and individuals) would continue or be enough to cover the needs of the students which, after the foundation year, was expanded to include the needs of all Aboriginal students on campus. At the end 1984, only $435 remained of the $10,500 originally donated. Seeking to ensure the continuation of the welfare fund, and to extend its reach to include scholarships for MOSA graduates, Ricklefs and Brown ventured into the corporate world. They had immediate success with BP. In 1988 and again in 1989, BP contributed $25,000 to the welfare fund. BP's manager of Government and Public Affairs, Peter Robertson, went even further. He organised and hosted a luncheon with representatives from the corporate sector at BP House in November 1988 to showcase MOSA's achievements. Two MOSA students, Helen Curzon-Siggers and Trevor Pearce, were invited to speak along with Ricklefs and Brown. Brown had the corporate sponsors 'eating out of his hand', Ricklefs recalled. With his 'impeccable, polished, middle-class accent', he challenged the image of what 'an Aboriginal person was supposed to be like'. Within a year Coles Myer were supporting two scholarships ($5000 per student per year) for undergraduates who had completed the MOSA program, and Telecom Australia was providing a scholarship ($10,000 per year) for a MOSA graduate studying engineering. In 1989 BHP also contributed $25,000 to the welfare fund, and underwrote five more bridging scholarships for MOSA students.

At the end 1989 Ricklefs estimated that sixty Aboriginal students, including bridging students and undergraduates, would require assistance from the welfare fund the following year. In order to provide each student an appropriate amount of financial support – calculated to be $150 per month, plus $100 per semester for books – he anticipated a shortfall in funding of $87,000 which Hank Young (a retired farmer who subsequently set up a Charitable Trust for Aboriginal Education and Welfare) generously agreed to provide. As it turned out, twenty fewer Aboriginal students enrolled in 1990 than expected, and so

MOSA: CREATING OPPORTUNITIES

MOSA students and staff, including: (back row from left) Merle Ricklefs and Robin McNamee; (front row from left) Isaac Brown, Eve Fesl and Helen Curzon-Siggers
Source: Monash Archives
Photographer: Tony Miller

Young was only called upon to provide half this amount. Not to be put off, Young gifted part of the remainder to fund a Law teacher/tutor position at MOSA for the second half of 1990.

* * *

In April 1988 an Aboriginal Education Policy Task Force was appointed by the Minister for Employment, Education and Training, J.S. Dawkins, and the Minster for Aboriginal Affairs, Gerard Hand, to advise on 'all aspects of Aboriginal education in Australia, assess the findings of recent research and policy reports, and prepare priorities for the funding of existing programs and new initiatives'. Chaired by Paul Hughes, former chairperson of the National Aboriginal

Education Committee, the Task Force was the first stage in the development of a national policy on Aboriginal education. Reviewing the participation of Aboriginal people across all levels of education, the Task Force found the current 'situation totally unacceptable':

> It is an anathema, as we approach the final decades of the twentieth century, that a developed country like Australia has not managed to extend human rights that are as fundamental as the provision of a basic education to all children and young people in the nation.

Although participation rates had increased markedly over the previous two decades, this was 'only because the level of Aboriginal participation in education was miniscule' before. In 1988 Aboriginal people remained 'the most severely educationally disadvantaged group of people in Australia'. What was needed, the Task Force asserted, was an approach to education that reinforced (rather than suppressed) Aboriginal peoples' 'unique cultural identity', and which grew out of Aboriginal community engagement. Unless the Aboriginal community was 'fully involved in determining the policies and programs that [were] intended to provide appropriate education for their community', any new approach would fail.

With reference to higher education, the Task Force recommended that existing arrangements for encouraging Aboriginal participation be reviewed, especially the effectiveness of support services. It further recommended that such services should:

> include effective bridging course arrangements which are targeted at the range of professional and other study areas in an institution, and which include both core units in academic preparation and study skills and specialized study units leading to chosen career outcomes.

MOSA: CREATING OPPORTUNITIES

Ricklefs, pouring over the Task Force report, wrote '= MOSA' in the margin beside this statement. Building on the Task Force report, a 'National Aboriginal and Torres Strait Islander Education Policy' was launched in October 1989 and implemented the following year. It introduced mainstream funding for Aboriginal participation in higher education on a rolling triennial basis. This provided much needed continuity for MOSA, however, it also had the effect of reducing its viability in the face of increased competition.

While the national policy on Aboriginal education was being developed, the Commonwealth government announced in November 1988 that it would provide over ten million dollars for equity initiatives under its Higher Education Equity Program commencing in 1989. Invited to make a submission, Ricklefs proposed to increase MOSA's annual intake to 40–60 new candidates each year by introducing a Recruitment Officer whose responsibility would be to find, counsel and encourage promising candidates. His request for Commonwealth funding was denied, but Ricklefs convinced the University to back his plan. Richard Jameson, a MOSA graduate with a Bachelor of Social Work degree, was appointed to the position of MOSA Recruitment Officer in 1990.

The number of students enrolling in MOSA had never been as high as anticipated. After the foundation year in which enrollments were kept deliberately small, an annual intake of 20 students had been expected, but up to 1987 this had not been achieved. Each year a good number of people made enquiries and came to the selection week in December. However, between then and the beginning of studies in March, a substantial proportion decided not to proceed. While this could be, and was, seen as positive, in the sense that people who felt unable to adapt to the demands of university excluded themselves, it had the effect of making MOSA a very expensive program to run: per head, Ricklefs estimated that each MOSA student cost approximately double that of an undergraduate student in Arts. Following the introduction of the science-stream, student numbers grew to twenty-four in 1989, nineteen in humanities and five in science. However, of these, only ten humanities students and three science students finished the year. This trend continued, and in fact worsened over the following years.

The year 1990 was a poor one for MOSA, with a higher rate of failure than had ever been true in the past. In mid 1990, Brown resigned to take up a position at the newly established Northern Territory University. For him it was a matter of going home, yet the timing made it look like he was abandoning a scheme that he and Ricklefs had represented as being more successful than it now seemed. While the long and difficult search for Brown's successor was conducted, Nelson served as Acting Director of MOSA. In February 1991 John Austin was appointed to the position of Director. A Monash graduate, Austin had worked at the ARC during Bourke's time as Director, and had taught at Swinburne and Monash. He had also worked at the Aboriginal Development Commission, the Northern Land Council and the Conservation Commission of the Northern Territory. Sir Richard Eggleston thought him an excellent appointment, and Ricklefs and Nelson were also delighted to have him on board. It was not long, however, before cracks began to appear; Brown's shoes were big ones to fill. Conflict arose between Austin and several members of the MOSA staff, including Brown's former secretary, Juanita Page, whom Austin formally reprimanded in May 1991 for typing 'things that [were] critical of MOSA and the Director'. A grievance committee was appointed towards the end of the year and two MOSA teachers were redeployed, but the problems persisted. Early in 1992, Austin was suspended and later resigned.

Acting Director of MOSA, Dr Eve Fesl, implemented a number of procedural changes that helped to restore the stability of the program, but the damage caused during the period 1991–92 had wider effects. Reed recalled a meeting with Gary Foley in 1992 in which the long-time activist insisted on knowing 'Are you with Austin or against him?': Reed gave the right answer, and so the meeting went ahead. Later Foley publically accused Monash of misappropriating 'hundreds of thousands of dollars of Aboriginal education monies via phantom "Aboriginal" students', but his allegations proved groundless. In 1993, thirty applications for entry into MOSA were received. Fesl applied the rigorous selection criteria that MOSA was known for, and ten students were selected. Of these, one student withdrew on the first day of the academic year, and two subsequently withdrew for reasons of ill-health, leaving just seven students.

Accounting for this 'unacceptably low' rate of enrollment, Sue Campbell, Associate Professor of Law and Chair of the MOSA Committee from 1993, pointed to the 'negative perceptions of MOSA which [had] spread throughout the entire Aboriginal community' in the wake of Austin's suspension and resignation. Increased competition from new tertiary programs for Aboriginal and Torres Strait Islander people established across the country was also a factor. It was clear that changes to the recruitment process needed to be made. From 1994, MOSA was extended to include Aboriginal people aged eighteen and over with or without high school certificates, and greater emphasis was placed on attracting students from Victoria. In direct contrast to Ricklefs' approach of seeking students from far afield in order to reduce the demands of family, the new MOSA

Director, Helen Curzon-Siggers (later Bnads), felt that a 'national strategy' for students was unwise. In her view, travelling away from home for study was 'not advantageous' to most Aboriginal and Torres Strait Islander people whose sense of loneliness when separated from kinship networks created 'emotional problems' that deflected from the focus of study.

One of the issues that contributed to the difficulties of 1991 was the lack of clear management, supervisory and reporting guidelines for the MOSA Director. Ricklefs and Brown had worked so well together that this had not come up as an issue until after Brown left. A solution was found in the creation of a new position, Head of Aboriginal Programs, designed to formally recognise and institutionalise Ricklefs' coordinating role in overseeing the budgetary allocation between MOSA, the Gippsland Centre for Koori Studies and the Koori Research Centre, and provide line-management support for the MOSA Director. As Head of Aboriginal Programs, Ricklefs oversaw the creation of statements of MOSA's Vision, Goals and Strategies that helped to redefine and clarify the program's role and objectives moving forward. He also drafted Monash's 'Aboriginal Education Strategy Plan'.

Under the National Aboriginal Education Policy, all universities were required to develop Aboriginal education strategies as part of their profile documentation. In Monash's case, compiling the document helped to bring together the various strands that had surfaced in the wake of the merger with the Gippsland Institute of Advanced Education and Chisholm Institute of Technology, and make a virtue of their disparate approaches. Highlighting 'the wide range of styles' covered by Monash's Aboriginal programs, Ricklefs pointed out that while Gippsland offered a 'community-based Associate Diploma course tailored to meet local Aboriginal needs', MOSA provided access to mainstream tertiary award courses at all Monash campuses. In drafting the strategy plan, Ricklefs identified a need for an Aboriginal liaison officer at the former Chisholm campuses of Caulfield and Frankston, and Sonia Smallcombe, a MOSA graduate with a degree in Arts, was appointed.

Ricklefs left Monash in 1993 to take up a position as Director of the Research School of Pacific Studies at the ANU. The responsibility of Head of Aboriginal Programs was given to Professor Lachlan Chipman, Pro Vice-Chancellor (Gippsland). Fesl resigned as Acting Director of MOSA in April that year, and left the University soon after. Her assistant, Helen Curzon-Siggers, was promoted to Acting Director of MOSA. Curzon-Siggers knew MOSA intimately having been a student in its third-intake in 1986. She went on to study in the Arts Faculty and was awarded her BA degree in 1991. Following the award of her degree, she reflected that MOSA had taught her 'to confront the past and just basically "get on with it" – attack wholeheartedly the future'. Within days of her promotion Curzon-Siggers 'opened direct communication with all areas of the MOSA unit', and arranged weekly meetings with staff and students, both MOSA and Aboriginal undergraduates. The result on the morale of the unit was felt immediately.

'New MOSA'

Curzon-Siggers' appointment as Acting Director (later Director) of MOSA ushered in a new period of stability for the program in terms of leadership, but turbulence in other areas continued. During the first half of 1994, the ABC's current affairs television program *The 7.30 Report* dealt MOSA's reputation a further damaging blow. Based on claims made by former and current students, *The 7.30 Report* alleged that MOSA was not achieving its stated aim of producing Aboriginal graduates, and criticised the unit for failing to provide adequate support for Aboriginal undergraduates. The University was criticised over its use of Commonwealth funds for Aboriginal students, and for failing to employ Aboriginal teaching staff. Although Campbell was able to refute most of *The 7.30 Report*'s allegations, the impact of her rejoinder was limited by its focus on technical matters of nuance and detail.

The 7.30 Report's criticisms provided an opportunity to take stock of MOSA's achievements, and think of new ways of promoting it to the general public. Towards the end of 1994, a logo was developed which signified the 'new MOSA'. The design, an earthworm image with 'several tracks – one pathway', was Curzon-Siggers' idea. Each concentric circle represented a different aspect of the MOSA family – students from various backgrounds, the university, the MOSA enclave; the dots represented the MOSA teachers and staff; and the lines represented the steps to achievement. Applied to specially designed posters, brochures, plaques, t-shirts, tablecloths, and stationery, and coupled with the slogan 'Creating Opportunities', the MOSA earthworm logo was an important first step in the rebranding of MOSA as a relevant and important provider of pre-tertiary education for Aboriginal people. More than that, according to Curzon-Siggers, it symbolised 'the commencement of a sense of identity for all those connected with the MOSA unit'.

MOSA received a further boost in 1995 with the graduation of two students as Bachelors of Law. Both students entered MOSA as mature age women and completed Bachelor of Arts degrees before commencing Law. Their achievements in the face of considerable personal difficulties were a great source of pride to MOSA staff and inspiration to MOSA students.

There was no doubt that MOSA in the mid 1990s was a different program from the one that commenced a decade earlier, 'the needs of the Aboriginal community [having] dictated changes in the subjects that were taught'. In 1994, in response to student requests for the inclusion of business management in the MOSA program, Curzon-Siggers hired a new teacher and changed the curriculum. However, despite the new course, the new image and the best efforts of the Director and staff, the numbers of students completing MOSA kept dropping. Twenty-four students commenced the bridging program in 1994, but only fourteen completed. When eleven out of twenty-two students withdrew from study before the middle of the following year, leaving none enrolled in the science stream, Curzon-Siggers was forced to temporarily suspend the science program. The next year, with no students interested in enrolling in science, Campbell and Curzon-Siggers decided that 'the time has come to acknowledge that the MOSA Science program has not succeeded'. Student numbers had always been low, and very few who passed the two-year course went on to study science at university. By contrast, the new business management course seemed to be thriving. Expanded into a stream parallel to the humanities stream in 1996, that year eight out of thirteen students elected to take Business Studies. The number who sat for final exams told a different story, however: only seven students, three in Business Studies and four in Humanities, completed the year.

Persistently low student numbers could not be ignored. During 1995 and 1996 hard questions were asked by members of the MOSA Committee about recruitment, retention and success rates. No-one doubted that Curzon-Siggers was doing all she could to promote the program and retain students, but it was clear that something was not working. Speaking from the vantage point of his association with MOSA over ten years, Andrew Markus queried 'the success of the unit of terms of available Aboriginal dollars', and asked whether some of the students admitted to MOSA 'should be in the course at all'. While he advocated 'a more rigourous selection' process, other members of the Committee favoured streaming the less-able students into an expanded two-year Humanities program. But this was not what students wanted. Among the reasons noted for MOSA's low rate of enrolment was a preference for 'the TAFE system of education, where HECS fees was not an issue'. Coupled with the fact that there were now similar programs to MOSA 'in each state and people [were] not prepared to leave their birth state of origin', it meant that MOSA had fewer students to choose from.

When MOSA began, it was the only university offering a pre-tertiary bridging program. Now there were so many options for Aboriginal students seeking tertiary education that MOSA's recruitment drive consisted of a 'roadshow', with Monash one of numerous institutions competing for Aboriginal students from a dwindling pool. Seeking ways to extend MOSA's influence and relevance, Curzon-Siggers instigated an active program of community outreach. MOSA teachers were sent to schools to give lectures on Aboriginal history and culture, and Aboriginal community members were invited to MOSA to view the program for themselves.

Within the university, Curzon-Siggers, who had worked as a nurse before enrolling in MOSA, began teaching an innovative Indigenous Health option to 3rd Year Medical students. At the same time, she began recasting MOSA as more than a bridging course, highlighting its role a 'resource centre' and stressing that MOSA acted a 'central point of information for the general community':

> The MOSA Unit provides the focus for a safe place of inquiry and an encouraging environment for non-Aboriginal people to meet and communicate with Indigenous students and staff. In terms of genuine reconciliation between black and white Australians, MOSA is the conduit and facilitator of necessary and positive change.

In support of reconciliation, information packs on Indigenous issues were produced at MOSA during 1997 and distributed to departments in the Faculty of Arts. That year students from the Business Management Course opened a MOSA shop on the 2nd floor of the Gallery Building selling goods made exclusively by Australian Indigenous people, including: boomerangs, carved emu eggs, silk scarves, didgeridoos and tablecloths.

Curzon-Siggers' positive attitude, energy and absolute devotion to MOSA held the unit together, but even she could not ignore the fact that its primary purpose was no longer being met. In March 1997, she took on the additional duties of Director of the Koorie Research Centre. In May Professor Colin Bourke and Associate Professor Eleanor Bourke commenced a review of Monash's Aboriginal Programs. As discussed in the following chapter, the consultants concluded that a 'more rational use of resources' was called for. There was no denying that MOSA was over-resourced and under-achieving. In addition to Curzon-Siggers, MOSA employed five teachers and three general staff members for a cohort of seven students in 1997, only six of whom sat the end of year exams. The Bourkes recommended that MOSA's staffing levels be significantly reduced, and that a student enrolment of twenty be MOSA's target for

1998. Recognising the need for change, Curzon-Siggers embraced the Bourkes' recommendations; she looked 'forward with enthusiasm to 1998 and directing the modifications to the MOSA program'. This opportunity, however, was denied to her. When only nine applications were received for admission to MOSA in 1998, the bridging program was suspended and eventually disbanded.

MOSA served an important purpose. For most of the students who completed the one or two-year program, its effect was transformative. Even some of those who did not complete the program found their lives, and the lives of their children, changed by the program and the opportunities it presented. While the lack of sustained growth over its fourteen-year lifespan suggests that it was not the great success its founders hoped and claimed it to be, its role in introducing hundreds of Aboriginal people to tertiary education cannot be denied or discounted. Aboriginal engagement with university education is a complex issue: the question of whether to seek recruits from far afield, as Ricklefs and Brown thought, or locally as Curzon-Siggers argued, symbolised this complexity. Cultural and kinship issues justified both approaches and neither was more or less successful. In the end, falling enrolments made it clear that the Aboriginal community 'wanted different types of educational avenues'. With MOSA out of business, the University was forced to seek other ways to bridge the educational divide.

Chapter 5

REBUILDING POTENTIAL, 1997–2014

Recognising the power of research as a tool for reform, Monash academics were at the forefront of change in Aboriginal Affairs during the 1960s and 1970s, leading the way with research on contemporary issues of Aboriginal employment, education, health and law. During the 1980s, with the establishment of MOSA and commencement of pre-tertiary education for Indigenous students, Monash again led the way. Its two Indigenous programs became three when the University amalgamated with the Gippsland Institute of Advanced Education in 1990. No longer a lone voice, by then most universities were teaching Aboriginal Studies and many were establishing Indigenous research centres of their own. Poorly resourced, Monash's Indigenous programs got left behind. By the mid 1990s, the KRC's profile had shrunk to such an extent that even Monash's own undergraduates were unaware of its existence.

Beginning with the review conducted by Professor Colin Bourke and Associate Professor Eleanor Bourke in 1997, this chapter examines structural and other changes that have helped Monash regain much of its former standing in Indigenous research, teaching, employment and development. Unlike the Centre's early history when change tended to be initiated and directed by individuals (at the will of government), in the recent past change has been mainly top-down, directed by Monash's senior management. Strong individuals with clear visions still run the programs, however increased recognition of the vital importance of Indigenous research and teaching, not just in terms of revenue (although this cannot be ignored as a factor) but in terms of the Universities' responsibility to Aboriginal and Torres Strait Islander people and contribution to reconciliation, is now apparent. Fifty-years after Colin Tatz persuaded the University to let him conduct research into contemporary Aboriginal Affairs in a formalised setting, building effective Indigenous programs has become a University-wide priority.

The Bourke Report

In 1997 Professor David Robinson, Monash's newly appointed Vice Chancellor, invited Colin Bourke, Professor and Dean of the Faculty of Aboriginal and Islander Studies, University of South Australia, and Associate Professor Eleanor Bourke, Director of the Aboriginal Research Institute, University of South Australia, to undertake a review of Monash's Indigenous programs. Robinson, who had been Vice Chancellor of the University of South Australia before coming to Monash, recognised the Bourkes' talent for building up and maintaining strong Aboriginal programs; he hoped they could do the same for Monash.

The review commenced mid year and was completed by October. The consultants were given a broad brief. Tasked with investigating the effectiveness – 'strengths, weaknesses, successes, and failures' – of Monash's three Aboriginal programs, they interviewed all staff members involved with the Koorie Research Centre (KRC), the Monash Orientation Scheme for Aborigines (MOSA), and the

Centre for Koorie Studies at Gippsland (GCKS). Appropriate senior and middle management of the University were also interviewed. The outcome was a series of recommendations that, while acknowledging the strong commitment of staff to their roles and widespread support for Aboriginal programs throughout the University, concluded that the programs were 'failing to meet their potential'. Monash's ability to make a 'significant contribution to Koori research, development and education' was noted on the first page of the report. The University had been the 'first ... to realize that Indigenous Australians required specific programs and organizational arrangements', but it had 'lost its pre-eminent position due to a range of factors'. The Bourkes' purpose was to 'provide advice which would enable the programs to achieve their potential in the future', thereby helping Monash 'to regain a reputation for being the leading Australian university' in Indigenous education and research.

University statistics showed that 206 Indigenous students were enrolled across various faculties and campuses in 1996. Of these, only 60 were known to staff involved in Monash's three Aboriginal programs. If the statistics were correct, this meant that the majority of Indigenous students at Monash were not receiving the benefit of specialised student support. The Bourke's first recommendation addressed this problem head-on: they called for a database to be established which included the individual names, courses, modes of enrollment, and contact details of all Indigenous students at Monash.

The Bourkes made separate recommendations concerning each of Monash's Aboriginal programs. Their perspective on MOSA, as noted in the previous chapter, was that it was overstaffed and under-enrolled. They recommended a minimum student enrollment of twenty, and that staffing be reduced. They also proposed that the curriculum be revised to better meet the needs of students. They did not recommend that the program be cut. To the contrary, they suggested that MOSA 'be broadened to include responsibility for Indigenous student support' across the whole University, and be renamed Monash Orientation *and Support* for Aborigines (thereby retaining the acronym MOSA). However, when student enrollments failed to reach their target the following year, MOSA was suspended and eventually disbanded.

Where the Bourkes wanted major change was in the area of undergraduate teaching and research. They recommended devolving Koorie Studies at Clayton to a centralised teaching unit at Gippsland as this would 'enable rationalization of resources and improved co-operation'. More than that, it would allow the KRC to concentrate on research, consultancy and post-graduate teaching. Being presently devoid of 'any long term strategies for research development', the Bourkes recommended the KRC 'undertake a review of research opportunities in Victoria, and elsewhere, in preparation for developing a rolling three year Research Strategic Plan'. As for Gippsland, their proposal to combine Koorie Studies there was designed to transform a unit which they plainly considered was underperforming. Gippsland offered a Diploma of Arts (Koorie Studies) to mainly Aboriginal students. Non-Aboriginal students were permitted to enroll in designated subjects by distance education. The Bourkes recommended opening the whole course to non-Aboriginal students, and encouraging additional Aboriginal students to enroll through distance education.

The major thrust of the Bourke Report was aimed at reorganising the current programs into a single coordinated unit. Previous attempts to align the programs had failed to produce lasting cohesion, the report noting a distinct 'lack of coordination between the programs with no senior staff direction to provide leadership, vision and coordination'. They recommended that the University amalgamate the existing programs into a 'Koorie Institute for Research, Development and Education'. They further recommended that a senior Indigenous academic be appointed at professorial level to provide leadership and oversight of the Institute, and that a Koori Advisory Committee be established to provide advice to the University and the Institute.

The final recommendations related to University-wide curriculum and Aboriginal education and employment strategies, and were closely aligned with Robinson's master plan for the university, *Leading the Way: The Monash Plan 1998–2002*. *Leading the Way* identified internationalisation of the curriculum as a key priority. All award programs were required to demonstrate within their curriculum a 'commitment to key internationalization outcomes'. The Bourkes wanted the same commitment shown to Aboriginalisation: they called for 'all appropriate Monash award programs to demonstrate a commitment to Aboriginalisation within the next triennium'. Perceiving no major problems with regard to Aboriginal employment, they called for current Aboriginal Employment Strategy to be maintained.

The Bourke Report was less a roadmap for change than a report card with suggested areas for improvement. Responses were generally positive with the recommendation to appoint an Indigenous professor attracting the most praise. Since the departure of Professor Merle Rickelfs, who had served as Monash's inaugural Head of Aboriginal Programs, the reporting and accountability structure of the three programs had been poor. Most respondents supported the establishment of the Koori Institute for Research, Development and Education, but not all agreed with its proposed name. Marlene Drysdale, Director of GCKS, suggested that 'Australian Indigenous' be substituted for 'Koori'; Dr Margaret James, the University's Equal Opportunity Manager, agreed. Echoing arguments against the use of Koori made by Bruce Knox and others in the late 1980s, James pointed out that the name was not appropriate for an Institute offering courses and conducting research on a full range of issues affecting Indigenous people throughout Australia.

The proposal to move the KRC's undergraduate teaching responsibilities to Gippsland also attracted criticism. Director of MOSA and the KRC, Helen Curzon-Siggers argued that nothing could match the 'Clayton model' of individual speakers and person-to-person contact with Aboriginal people. Drysdale was not happy either, but her objections related more to the consultants' suggestion that the GCKS was not pulling its weight. Describing the report as 'rushed', she complained that 'too many assumptions were made about the programs at Gippsland'. Peter Marshall, assistant general manager (personnel services), was 'somewhat disappointed with the level of analysis' devoted to Monash's Aboriginal employment strategy. He, like Drysdale, felt that perhaps the consultants did not have enough time to properly review Aboriginal employment matters. Given that Monash invested 'in excess of $50,000 each year in encouraging growth in the levels of Aboriginal employment', Marshall wanted to know whether the consultants considered this 'sufficient, or whether economies [could] be achieved through better mainstreaming of Aboriginal employment matters'. Historian Dr Marian Quartly, Dean of the Faculty of Arts, thought the report 'less than clear in several respects'. With characteristic brusqueness she asked: 'Which faculty will provide the academic home for the Koori teaching program? What ever it is? And, for that matter, the research program? What formal relationships are envisaged with the faculties?'

REBUILDING POTENTIAL, 1997–2014

Eleanor Bourke
Source: Australian Institute of Aboriginal and Torres Strait Islander Studies

Centre for Australian Indigenous Studies

These were all matters that would be resolved in time. Curzon-Siggers' five-year contract as Director of MOSA and the KRC expired at the end of 1998 and was not renewed. Emotionally and physically drained, Curzon-Siggers had no desire to continue in the role. After a short break, she started her own consultancy business before taking a position as Aboriginal Hospital Liaison Officer at the Southern Health Care Network. Pending the appointment of a senior Indigenous academic, Associate Professor Andrew Markus served as Acting Head of Aboriginal Programs. In 1998 the Monash Council approved a Chair of Australian Indigenous Studies within the Faculty of Arts. The following year Professor Eleanor Bourke was appointed to the Chair with dual responsibility as Director, Monash Aboriginal Programs.

Descended from the Wergaia and Wamba Wamba peoples of western Victoria, Eleanor Bourke (formerly Koumalatsos, née Anderson) was a strong advocate of the benefits of education for Aboriginal people. Leading by example, she completed a Diploma of Arts (RMIT), Bachelor of Arts (CCAE), and Masters of Education (University of Adelaide) and was enrolled as a PhD candidate at the time of her appointment. Her association with Monash began in the late 1970s when, as Aboriginal Student Liaison officer at the University of Melbourne, she began working with then Director of the ARC, Colin Bourke, facilitating the delivery of Black Studies lectures at the University of Melbourne. She later served on the Board of the ARC. Her return to Monash in 1999 was well received. She oversaw the disestablishment of the KRC, the GCKS and MOSA, and establishment of the Centre for Australian Indigenous Studies (CAIS) in the Faculty of Arts.

CAIS consolidated the three antecedent Aboriginal programs into a single unit comprising teaching, research and Indigenous support. Contrary to the Bourke Report, Indigenous Studies continued to be taught from Clayton and Gippsland. A new first-year sequence, Introduction to Australian Indigenous Studies I & II, was introduced which enabled students to undertake a major or minor in Indigenous Studies at either campus. At second and third year, students could choose from a range of electives, including: Land Rights and Native Title; Australian Aboriginal Women; Australian Indigenous Health; Human Rights and the Indigenous Australian Experience; Aboriginal People and the Law, Archeology of Indigenous Australia; and Tourism and Indigenous Australia. CAIS at Clayton offered an honours program and a Masters by research program. CAIS at Gippsland hosted a Junior University program – a four-day orientation for Year 11 and 12 Indigenous students designed to introduce prospective students to university life – and plans were in place for the introduction of a two-year full-time Diploma in Arts (Australian Indigenous Studies) for Indigenous students with Year 11 (or mature age entry) at Clayton and Gippsland.

An Indigenous Student Support Unit was established within CAIS which provided assistance to prospective students, ongoing support to Indigenous students enrolled in all courses at all campuses of Monash, and arranged individual tutoring assistance under the Aboriginal Tutorial Assistance Scheme. Clayton-based students had access to the Elizabeth Eggleston Library (formerly Memorial Resource Centre) which now held over 4000 monographs, journals and audio-visual materials. In 2000 Bourke won a large Australian Research Council infrastructure grant ($101,000) to catalogue the Eggleston Library and establish links with the main library. That year the federal member for Chisholm and Monash alumna, Anna Burke, praised CAIS's 'fantastic work' in a speech in the House of Representatives. CAIS was not only a 'centre for learning and research', she enthused, but 'a meeting place ... where Indigenous students can relax, feel at home and get support and counseling from the friendly and accessible, if overworked, staff'.

The Centre was functioning well. In January 2001 Bourke gave notice of her intention to retire; she left the University in June. CAIS Senior Research Fellow, Dr Lynette Russell, was appointed Acting Director. When the position of CAIS Director and Chair of Indigenous Studies was advertised later that year, she applied and was successful. Russell grew up in a working-class outer Melbourne suburb. Like many Aboriginal families trying to survive in the face of relentless persecution and legalised discrimination, hers passed as white. So effective was her family's passing that Russell was unaware of her Aboriginal heritage until the 1980s. Then studying archeology at La Trobe University, she shifted her attention to history, gaining a PhD from the University of Melbourne in 1995. Her thesis, '(Re)presented pasts: historical and contemporary constructions of Australian Aboriginalities', was later published as *Savage Imaginings* (2001). She worked as a lecturer at the Institute of Koorie Education at Deakin University, and held a Faculty of Arts Post-doctoral Fellowship in the School of Historical Studies, Monash University, prior to joining CAIS.

Continuing a process commenced under Bourke, one of the first things Russell did when she took over as Director of CAIS was to check that all the students listed as Indigenous were actually Indigenous. She ran her 'finger down the list of students' and found a significant number who appeared to be international students. Assuming that most had probably misunderstood the question at enrollment, she instituted a 'double checking mechanism' – 'we rang every student' – and the numbers dropped: 'it looked on paper as though I managed to cut the numbers in half', she recalled. The University's senior managers were not pleased: 'Central didn't like it … the Vice Chancellor did not like it'. However, since the University received government funding based on the number of Aboriginal and Torres Strait Islander students enrolled, Russell felt it was important to get the figures right. She was not prepared to take money on 'false pretenses'; she wanted to be able 'to sleep at night'. The number of Indigenous students at Monash fluctuated over the next few years, but remained low: from a 'real base' of 98 in 2002, it dropped to 92 in 2005 before rising to 116 in 2007.

That year Monash ranked eighth in the Group of Eight (Go8) universities for Indigenous Access. One of the University's Key Performance Indicators, Indigenous Access referred to the number of Indigenous students and staff on campus. Seeking ways to improve its ranking, the Vice Chancellor, Robinson, established an Indigenous Access and Support Programs Task Force to explore different strategies for Indigenous recruitment. The Task Force made it clear that while Monash's Indigenous engagement initiatives were broader than CAIS – for example, in 2006 the Indigenous Health Unit of the School of Rural Health at Monash, in collaboration with James Cook University and the University of New South Wales, undertook a project to identify strategies for improvement in the recruitment of Indigenous medical students – CAIS needed to be better supported in order to achieve better results.

The main obstacle to recruitment continued to be the low number of Year 12 completions among Indigenous students: in 2005, the Year 12 retention rate for Indigenous students nationally was 39.5 percent compared to 76.6 percent for non-Indigenous students. Since increasing this number would increase the pool of potential applicants to Monash, the Task Force focused its attention on ways of encouraging Indigenous students to finish Year 12. It examined the efforts of several other Go8 universities and was sufficiently impressed by programs at the University of Sydney and the University of New South Wales to recommend that Monash follow their lead. At the University of Sydney a highly successful paid mentoring scheme paired Indigenous undergraduate students with Indigenous high school students. Relationships were developed over a number of years, providing academic as well as other types of support. Taking a different approach, UNSW ran an Indigenous Winter School, Nura Gili, for Indigenous students in Years 10–12. A one-week residential program, Nura Gili was credited with lifting UNSW from 8th to 5th position in the Go8 for Indigenous Access. The Task Force recommended that CAIS develop similar programs, and that renewed attention be given to creating entry pathways to university for Indigenous students without Year 12, or with low Year 12 scores. In particular, the Task Force suggested the possibility of offering Year 12 equivalent enabling courses through Monash College, a provider of pathways for international students. As discussed below, many of these ideas were taken up by the Yulendj Indigenous Engagement Unit (established in 2011).

The Task Force concluded that CAIS's effectiveness was limited by its organisational structure, especially its 'bottom heavy' staffing profile. Russell was effectively Director of two separate units within CAIS, one responsible for academic matters (teaching and research), and the other for access and support, yet her only administrative assistance came from junior- to middle-level professional staff. The Task Force proposed the appointment of a senior administrator who would be responsible for driving the strategic direction of the Support Unit. It also suggested that the Support Unit, while remaining within CAIS and under Russell's oversight, report to the Deputy Vice-Chancellor (Education) and have its own budget. These changes were implemented in 2008.

On 13 February 2008 Prime Minister Kevin Rudd formally apologised to Australia's Indigenous people, particularly those affected by child removal policies. Within days, the Council of Monash responded with the following resolution:

> Monash University is fifty years old this year. But its half-century cannot compare with the tens of thousands of years in which Indigenous Australians have walked, lived and flourished across the breadth and length of Australia.
>
> Echoing the sentiments of apology and partnership affirmed by the Prime Minister, Monash reaffirms its role to advance the educational and career aspirations of Indigenous Australians.
>
> This will occur on every one of Monash's eight campuses – metropolitan, regional and international – and in our staffing, educational and research programs.

Giving effect to the Council's resolution, recently appointed Deputy Vice-Chancellor (Education), Professor Adam Shoemaker, convened a series of three roundtable discussions during May and June 2008. All Indigenous staff and students at Monash were invited, and invitations were also extended to non-Indigenous students, staff and the wider community. The roundtables were well attended with 25–50 people present at each session. At Shoemaker's request, Helen Fletcher-Kennedy, a non-Indigenous senior administrator, took note of everything that was said. Fletcher-Kennedy recalled Shoemaker telling her before the first roundtable that 'in this space you need to listen ... listen carefully and observe'; she 'didn't say a word'.

A Canadian-born scholar of indigenous literature and culture, Shoemaker was another 'outsider' who saw Indigenous disadvantage as a wrong to be righted. Given university-wide responsibility for Indigenous matters, he viewed the roundtables as a starting point for change. They resulted in a set of five initiatives designed to demonstrate and publically promote Monash's recognition of, and respect for, Indigenous history, culture and heritage:

1. Ensure that each campus of the University signifies, symbolically and publically, the University's commitment to Indigenous

people, by flying both the Aboriginal and Torres Strait Islander flags.
2. Implement an appropriate custom for Graduation ceremonies whereby Indigenous staff and students are offered the opportunity to wear a stole, sash or other tricolor garment in traditional colours to signify their cultural heritage and the University's recognition of it.
3. Ensure that NAIDOC week, National Sorry Day, and other Indigenous days of significance are formally noted in the student diary and the University's Cultural Calendar. Establish a centrally organized and supported University-wide celebration of NAIDOC week as an annual even on the University calendar.
4. Establish an annual Indigenous Welcome Day where elders and traditional custodians are hosted at a lunch or dinner gathering by members of Council and members of senior management.
5. Incorporate local Aboriginal language elements, and references to traditional custodians, on the University website.

The University Council endorsed the initiatives in 2009. In the same year the Victorian State Government passed the *Monash Act 2009*. Under this Act, Monash was required to:

f. use its expertise and resources to involve Aboriginal and Torres Strait Islander people of Australia in its teaching, learning, research and advancement of knowledge activities and thereby contribute to:

> i. realizing Aboriginal and Torres Strait Islander aspirations; and
>
> ii. the safeguarding of the ancient and rich Aboriginal and Torres Strait Islander cultural heritage.

Appreciating the significance of the moment, Shoemaker wasted no time in implementing the roundtables' suggestions.

Flying the Aboriginal and Torres Strait Islander flags at every campus helped to identify and affirm Monash as a 'culturally safe place for all Indigenous people'. The flags and stoles, together with the other initiatives listed above, were enabling steps which allowed Monash to move toward its desired (and legislated) goal of improved access for Indigenous people to all aspects of university life. The establishment of an Aboriginal garden at the Clayton campus also helped. Botanist Dr Beth Gott from the School of Biological Sciences hoped the garden, which featured a range of plants known to have been used for food, medicine, fibre or tools by Aboriginal people in south-eastern Australia, would encourage non-Indigenous people 'to experience a connection with the land'.

The next step was the establishment of an Indigenous Advisory Council. Under the chairmanship of Professor Colin Bourke, the IAC set up a Strategic Working Group to consider the processes required for achieving improved access for Indigenous staff and students at Monash. The Working Group identified four key areas of Indigenous related activity: Indigenous Studies (research and teaching); Indigenous Student Access, Recruitment and Support; Indigenous Employment and Development; Indigenous Community Engagement. The Working Group advocated a 'whole-of-university' approach to achieving improved Indigenous access and pointed to a lack of Indigenous staff and resources focused exclusively on achieving this. It also highlighted what it saw as a misalignment of organisational structures and accountabilities, for while the overall responsibility for Indigenous access and participation rested with the portfolio of the DVCE, the unit primarily engaged in the business of Indigenous student access, recruitment and support, as well as teaching and research, CAIS, was aligned with the Faculty of Arts.

This created numerous headaches. The biggest problem, as far as Fletcher-Kennedy was concerned, was that it was 'very, very difficult to have the staff within an Arts Faculty ... telling a Business faculty or a Medicine faculty what they needed to be doing with Indigenous students'.

Fletcher-Kennedy was referring to the staff of the Indigenous Student Support Unit located within CAIS. The appointment of a senior administrator to look after the ISSU had eased Russell's workload giving her more time to focus on the academic side of CAIS's work, but she was effectively still doing two jobs. Russell and CAIS's academic staff were focused on building CAIS's reputation as a research and teaching centre. A strong advocate of research-led teaching – 'otherwise you're a high school, you're teaching what other people have put in text books' – Russell had developed an Indigenous Studies curriculum around the research interests of CAIS's staff. However, with low to very low enrolments across all units, few honours students and negligible numbers of international students, it was apparent that something needed to change. In 2010 Russell commissioned Professor Ian Lilley from the Aboriginal and Torres Strait Islander Studies Unit at the University of Queensland to conduct a review of CAIS's curriculum. Lilley interviewed CAIS teaching and research staff, and carried out a detailed assessment of CAIS's unit offerings. His report identified the absence of a 'coherent plan purpose-designed to achieve an unambiguous end-goal' as one of the Centre's main weaknesses. A 'thorough renewal' of CAIS's entire academic program was needed, Lilley asserted, one in which CAIS staff 'had a long, hard look at what they teach, why and how, to ensure that all staff and students share a clear idea of what the academic program is for and how staff and students should go about achieving this end'. Lilley also recommended separating CAIS's academic program from the support unit to form a stand-alone teaching and research entity.

In light of Lilley's report and in keeping with the IAC's Strategic Working Group's recommendations, Shoemaker decided to establish a stand alone Indigenous Engagement Unit at the end of 2010. For Russell, the split seemed to come out of nowhere: she thought it extremely ill-conceived and poorly executed. She recalled how, 'literally one afternoon, I was told I was no longer in charge of student support'. It was not meant as a slight, nor as a criticism of her work, but that was how it felt. At the same time, it was a relief. Looking back on 2010, Russell remembers sagging under the weight of work and responsibility. On reflection, she acknowledged that everything 'worked out quite well', but at the time it was very difficult not to take the division of CAIS personally.

Yulendj: 'A Slow Revolution'

Clearly demarcating the line between what had formerly been two units within CAIS, the academic (teaching and research) program was renamed the Monash Indigenous Centre (MIC), and the new program devoted to Indigenous recruitment, engagement and support was given an Aboriginal name, Yulendj, a Kulin word for knowledge and intelligence. Formally established on 1 January 2011, Yulendj brought together staff of the Indigenous Student Support Unit and staff of the Office of the DVCE into a single, centrally funded hub with a university-wide remit. Headed by Fletcher-Kennedy, the Yulendj Indigenous Engagement Unit was housed in the Gallery Building alongside the MIC until 2014 when MIC moved to the 8th floor of the Menzies Building.

MAKING A DIFFERENCE

Staff at Yulendj Indigenous Engagement Unit. From left to right: Cathy Doe, Jason Brailey, Helen Fletcher-Kennedy, Aunty Diane Singh, Angela Estcourt, Kristel Keleher, and Brian Walker on the occasion of Monash receiving a Wurreker Award for University Pathways (October, 2014)
Source: Helen Fletcher-Kennedy

One of the first steps Fletcher-Kennedy took in her new role was to establish the position of 'Elder in Residence', a continuing appointment split between Yulendj and MIC that Aunty Diane Singh has held since 2011. A MOSA graduate (1991 intake), Singh worked at CAIS for many years in a number of different roles including as Community Liaison Officer. Her three daughters all attended Monash, and one of her grand-daughters attended the 'Hands On Monash Camp' in 2015 (see below). Singh's experience, which exemplifies the level of intergenerational involvement made possible by the University's long commitment to Indigenous programs, makes her an invaluable resource and role model to Indigenous staff and students.

Taking a rights-based approach to facilitating University objectives, Yulendj's core business was (and is) students. While it also devoted considerable time and resources to community engagement and Indigenous staff employment and development, the main challenge inherited by Yulendj was to create new opportunities to increase the number of Indigenous students at Monash. The University's track record for retention and completion was good; the problem lay in getting Indigenous students to come to Monash in the first place. The number of universities in Victoria alone – nine in 2011 – made for a highly competitive environment. Working directly with secondary schools, Yulendj developed a range of new programs including 'Hands on Monash Camp', a three-day camp held at Clayton, and 'Experience Monash Day', an annual event attracting hundreds of Indigenous students from schools across Victoria to Clayton, which managed to boost undergraduate enrolments of Indigenous students from 69 in 2011, to over 100 in 2014. Total enrolments of indigenous students across all course types over the same period increased from 117 to 152, a growth rate of 29 percent.

Building on the work done in recruitment, Yulendj created pathways to ensure prospective students were given the means and opportunity to succeed. In 2011 an Indigenous Enabling Program (IEP) was set up to widen access while ensuring academic preparedness. A partnership with Monash College was forged which enabled Indigenous IEP students to meet the prerequisites for a wide range of degrees including Science, Nursing, Emergency Health, Education, Business and Economics, and Information Technology. Although only small numbers were involved (in 2014, seven students enrolled into an IEP, six completed the course, and five enrolled at Monash), the individual care and attention each student received from staff at Yulendj ensured a high retention rate; much higher than expected. The successor, in many ways, to

MOSA, the IEP encountered the same type of mindset regarding the 'lowering of university standards' when it began. Locating the IEP outside the University (at Monash College) helped to reduce the risk for 'standards focused people', Fletcher Kennedy explained, none of whom 'expected that every student would get through as they are'. This 'sofly, softly' approach to change, working behind the scenes to create new pathways for small numbers of Indigenous students, sometimes individual students, was (and is) Yulendj's path to 'slow revolution'.

Growing student numbers at a sustainable level is only part of Yulendj's remit. The team of seven (all of whom, apart from Fletcher-Kennedy, are Indigenous) also ensures that Indigenous students receive adequate support during their time at Monash. Tutoring is offered to any Indigenous student who needs it. Jason Brailey, manager of Yulendj, is quick to point out that 'no-one gets into Monash who hasn't earned the right to be here, whether it's through direct entry or through a pathway', therefore most of the tutoring is 'not remedial'. He stresses that there is no 'scaffolding of Indigenous students' at Monash. Instead, for the most part, Indigenous tutoring is about boosting 'self-confidence ... [and] managing the transition into a pretty strange culture'. 'University culture is odd for everyone', Brailey quips, but for Indigenous students, the majority of whom are the first in their families to attend university, it can be a very 'isolating experience'. In 2013, nearly 70 percent of commencing Indigenous students at Monash were classed as 'first in family'. For such students, the support provided by Yulendj helps to fill in a range of sophisticated cultural gaps. Rightfully proud of Yulendj's role in transforming 'shy, little timid kids ... into awesome adults who go off and work in Aboriginal community organisations and do really good work', Brailey sees the Engagement Unit's role in providing a 'safe and comfortable place where they can build ... cultural pride' as one of its most important functions.

Yulendj is responsible for developing, promoting and facilitating 'cultural safety' training for staff and students. In 2013 it ran an Introduction to Indigenous Cultural Safety workshop involving over three-hundred staff, and in 2014 it launched an online cultural awareness program for students at Monash. Yulendj is also responsible for coordinating Monash's first Reconciliation Action Plan (RAP). Released in 2013, the RAP provides guidance in Indigenous education, research, employment outcomes, and community engagement, and forms part of Monash's Indigenous Strategic Framework. At its core is a statement of respect for Aboriginal and Torres Strait Islander peoples, cultures and knowledge, a commitment to working towards 'addressing the legacies of the past', and a 'desire to *make a difference*'. The latter, it is noted, 'informs everything we do'.

Yulendj's ability to facilitate certain RAP objectives, such as the requirement to build Indigenous viewpoints and content into curriculum, increase the number of Indigenous staff, both academic and professional, and increase opportunities within Monash to advance Aboriginal and Torres Strait Islander staff interests, is limited by a lack of resourcing and a lack of a senior Indigenous leadership in senior management roles. Yet, as Brailey observes, the resourcing of Yulendj is part of the ebb and flow of university life. Monash, like any complex organisation, has many competing interests, and it is up to Yulendj to demonstrate the need for additional resources; that is part of its job. Beyond such challenges lies a philosophical and arguably more fundamental problem of perception. For Brailey, it is a question of how Yulendj is seen by the broader University community.

He worries that once the gap in education, access and opportunity is closed, an argument will be made that units like Yulendj are no longer needed. Rather than surplus to requirement, Brailey insists that there will always be a need for 'Aboriginal places and spaces' on campus 'by virtue of the fact that it is Aboriginal land'. His vision is that Yulendj will evolve into a 'place of recognition'; 'a place where Aboriginal people can make from it what they will … a place of excellence in all sorts of different ways'.

Monash Indigenous Centre

Excellence is also high on Russell's agenda for the future. Conservative in her approach to change, she believes 'if it's not broken, don't fix it', and since the MIC 'doesn't seem broken' to her, her plans for the future revolve around enhancement rather than reform. Her ultimate vision is for the MIC to become the 'premier Indigenous Studies unit in Australia', a place 'known for its academic excellence'. With Russell in charge, this seems an achievable objective.

The Monash Indigenous Centre turned fifty in December 2014. Abroad at the time, Russell was a world away from the lone office at Clayton where the Centre began. Awarded a prestigious visiting fellowship at All Souls College, Oxford, she was ensconced in one of the wealthiest colleges at the oldest English-speaking university in the world. Her fellowship was (and is) a significant achievement for any academic, especially for an Indigenous academic, and is testament to the value she places on academic rigour and excellence. During her time as Chair of Indigenous Studies at Monash, Russell has published twelve books and countless articles and book chapters, won numerous small and large research grants, including an Australian Research Council Professorial Fellowship (2011–2016), and was recently elected a Fellow of the Academy of Social Sciences in Australia. Such extraordinary success often comes at a price. For Russell, the cost has been community engagement: she freely acknowledges that she is 'much less community focused' than previous Centre Directors. Yet, with Yulendj now responsible for community engagement, the cost is muted.

In 2014 MIC was staffed by a mixture of Indigenous and non-Indigenous academics and professional staff, and had a growing number of Indigenous and non-Indigenous HDR students. Russell, who 'talent spots' potential new recruits at conferences and seminars, is proud of what the MIC has achieved during her Directorship. She points especially to the 'bringing in of Anthropology and Archeology … and History and Performance Studies'. While still focusing on contemporary experiences and issues involving Aboriginal peoples, identities and culture, today MIC is a 'much more integrated and intellectually engaged space than ever before'. International perspectives inform much of the Centre's teaching and research. Driven less by the university-wide emphases on internationalisation, and more by Russell's conviction that students need to see and understand 'the kinds of experiences that Aboriginal and Torres Strait Islander people have as part of the global system of colonization', every MIC course includes an international comparative element. Strong partnerships and ongoing collaborations with individual researchers and research centres at universities in New Zealand, Europe and North America support this focus.

Conclusion: How Far Have We Come?

Have Monash's Indigenous programs made a difference in Aboriginal peoples' lives? The founder and inaugural director of the Centre for Research in Aboriginal Affairs, now the Monash Indigenous Centre, Professor Colin Tatz returned to Monash in 2014 to give his perspective on 'how far we've come'. Taking a long view, and commenting on a wide range of social indicators, Tatz concluded that basically 'we're kind of slow learners'. Despite all the advances and developments of the previous fifty years, Aboriginal people were still 'segregated enough in the political and bureaucratic minds, still removed enough from society, to impose restrictions on wages, on incomes, on income access, on food access, on alcohol access, and to being subject to special "mutual responsibility agreements"'. This meant that many Aboriginal people were 'still separated from the mainstream society and the services that are provided by the mainstream society'. In terms of legal equality, wage parity, health, and housing, some improvements had been made, but the overall picture remained one of gross disadvantage for Aboriginal people. For every 'win', symbolic or real, there were an equal or greater number of losses: Land Rights versus the 'institutionalization of Aboriginal youth'; fewer deaths due to tuberculosis, more due to heart disease and renal failure; the modern tragedy of Aboriginal suicide, which Tatz described as 'the social indicator to end all indicators'; and so on.

Yet it was not all doom and gloom. 'Fantastic' changes had occurred in the areas of education and academia. Whereas during the early 1960s Aboriginal people were 'objects of scientific curiosity' with academic interest limited to recording the last remnants of a people and a culture in decline, Tatz observed that the 'menu' had completely changed. Aboriginal people were now, and had been for some time, co-ventures in research, organising and running projects of their own design. And whereas in 1969 the number of Aborigines at university around the country could be counted on two hands (which, at the time, was an 'amazing' achievement, Tatz recalled), now there were dozens of Aboriginal doctors, lawyers, and hundreds of other tertiary educated Aboriginal professionals. The Monash Centre for Research into Aboriginal Affairs had played a role in initiating these changes which, Tatz concluded, ultimately made life better for Aboriginal people in 2014 than in 1964. All things considered, he reasoned that 'in terms of freedom; in terms of human rights; in terms of dignity, I'd rather be a young Aboriginal now than then'. When to this list is added the support provided by Yulendj and academic stimulation provided by MIC, it is likely that many of the nearly 200 Indigenous students enrolled at Monash in 2015 would probably agree. Led by people of exceptional character, skill and determination, the research, teaching, support and development conducted by Monash's Indigenous programs over fifty years have contributed to better understandings of the causes of Indigenous disadvantage which in turn have helped to improve the material circumstances of Indigenous peoples' lives. But there is still more work to be done.

DISCUSSION OF SOURCES

Historians love footnotes; I love them as much as anyone, yet this book has none. Why? There is a perception that the average interested reader is put off by footnotes, finding them either a distraction or a sign that the work is 'too academic'. I don't know whether this is true, but I am inclined to think that in a work of this nature, which seeks to reach as wide an audience as possible, their value is limited. Footnotes provide proof of the evidentiary basis of stories and information, protect writers of true stories from accusations of fabrication, and give future researchers a place to start; but, unless you are familiar with their form, they can be daunting and difficult to read.

This book is based on solid archival research. All the information is traceable back to a document in the archives, a government report, a newspaper article, an interview, or a secondary source. Rather than use conventional footnotes or endnotes, I have chosen to describe, in accessible prose, the main sources I used to write each chapter.

All the archival material comes from the Monash University Archives. The main source for the introduction, chapters 1, 2 and 3 was MON 1 Administrative Correspondence Files (CF/166/0 Parts 1–4). Comprising four densely packed folios, this series contains communication with the University's senior management about the CRAA from before it was established until 1985, copies of letters to and from government, copies of annual reports and minutes of Board meetings. Most of the documents relate to the Centre's early years, the quantity of correspondence and other material gradually petering out as staff and administrative practices changed in later decades. Supplementary archival material for chapter 3 came from MON 974 (File 88/0564), being material relating to the administration and operation of the Aboriginal Research Centre from 1987–1997, and MON 37, being minutes of the Board of the Koori Research Centre from 1970–1993. The letter that eluded me for six months was in MON 1073 Koori Research Centre Subject Files (file 2002/06/8 MOSA correspondence). Further archival material came from staff files, newspaper articles (Trove), and government reports (Parliament of Australia).

Chapter 4 draws on an incredibly rich set of records relating to the establishment and operation of the Monash Orientation Scheme for Aborigines preserved for posterity by Professor Merle Ricklefs. Aware of the significance of his undertaking, Ricklefs documented everything, keeping files on all members of MOSA's staff, correspondence relating to MOSA's inception, dealings with government, negotiations with corporate sponsors, press reports, minutes of staff meetings, Committee minutes, annual reports and so on. Ricklefs' highly ordered files (MON 546/561 MOSA Committee) – more than 60 of them – end with his departure from Monash in 1993. Insight into MOSA's final years comes from MON 1072: MOSA Committee: Agenda and Minutes, 1994–1998, a much less comprehensive, though still informative, collection.

The closer I came to the present, the thinner the archival files became. Chapter 5 draws on very few archival sources. The Bourke Report and responses came from RMO1998/1506 and RMO1997/0406, and documents relating to the reorganisation of Monash's Indigenous programs were in RMO1998/1507. Apart from these, I relied on records still in the custody of the Directors of the Monash Indigenous

DISCUSSION OF SOURCES

Centre and Yulendj Indigenous Engagement Unit (strategic plans, self-reviews, and other material relating to the current operation of these units), public documents, such as Monash's Reconciliation Action Plan 2013–14, and interviews.

I was privileged to have long conversations with numerous people involved in Monash's Indigenous programs: former Directors and Board members, MOSA teachers and students. Their reflections and recollections are interspersed throughout the book, providing colour and life. Associate Professor Louis Waller alerted me his obituary of Elizabeth Eggleston, and a second obituary by Charles Rowley, both published in the *Monash University Law Review* (Vol.3 1976), which provided much needed insight into Eggleston's personality and life. Colin Tatz's seminar, delivered on the 50th anniversary of the establishment of the CRAA, was recorded by Yulendj is available online: http://monash.edu/news/show/50-years-of-indigenous-engagement-at-monash. A typescript copy of Tatz's memoir, 'The Lion's Feathers: how I think I've lived', written mainly for his family and including more detail about his early life than the published version, was also used. Readers can also consult Tatz's published memoir, *Human Rights and Human Wrongs: A Life Confronting Racism* (Monash University Publishing, 2015).

Important social, cultural and political context, as well as historical interpretation and argument comes from the following works: Bain Attwood and Andrew Markus, *The Struggle for Aboriginal Rights: A Documentary History* (Allen & Unwin, 1999); Bain Attwood, *Rights for Aborigines* (Allen & Unwin, 2003); Jeremy Beckett, 'Aboriginality, Citizenship and Nation State', *Social Analysis* 24 (1988): 3–18; Richard Broome, *Fighting Hard: The Victorian Aborigines Advancement League* (Aboriginal Studies Press, 2015); Graeme Davison and

Kate Murphy, *University Unlimited: The Monash Story* (Allen & Unwin, 2012); Coral Dow and John Gardiner-Garden, 'Overview of Indigenous Affairs: Part 1, 1901–1991', Parliament of Australia, accessed 12 June 2015: http://www.aph.gov.au/about_parliament/parliamentary_departments/parliamentary_library/pubs/bn/1011/indigenousaffairs1; Lorna Lippmann, *Generations of Resistance: The Aboriginal Struggle for Justice* (Longman Cheshire, 1981); and Merridy Malin and Deborah Maidment, 'Education, Indigenous Survival and Well-Being: Emerging Ideas and Programs', *Australian Journal of Indigenous Education* 32 (2003): 85–99.

INDEX

Note: page references in bold indicate photographs.

Abnednego, Jacob 10
Aboriginal affairs, lack of research interest in 1960s 1, 15–16
Aboriginal art exhibition and workshop 51
Aboriginal Arts Board 50
'Aboriginal Arts' seminar 38
Aboriginal child removal 57, 69
'Aboriginal Child Survival' Seminar 57
Aboriginal Community College, Adelaide 89
Aboriginal Cooperative, Fitzroy 35
Aboriginal Development Commission 60
Aboriginal education
    Aboriginal colleges 70
    bilingual education programs 50
    bridging courses for university entry 81
    changing approaches to 88–89
    CRAA seminar 10
    development of national policy 107–9, 112
    dual aspects 44
    Monash's strategy for 112–13
    in pre-schools 11–12
    see also Aboriginal students
Aboriginal Education Policy Task Force (Cwlth) 107–9
'Aboriginal Education' seminar 10, 29
Aboriginal Education Strategy Plan, Monash 112–13
Aboriginal employment and training 79
Aboriginal flag 132
Aboriginal garden, Clayton campus 133
Aboriginal health journal 39
Aboriginal Health policy 29

'Aboriginal Health Services' seminar 18, 21, 28–29, 39
Aboriginal health study 8–9
Aboriginal history projects 50, 69
Aboriginal Issues: Health 40
Aboriginal languages
    course in Pitjantjatara 53
    study of viii
    in Victorian schools 51, 56, 63
Aboriginal pastoral workers 9
Aboriginal plant foods 65
Aboriginal population of Victoria, statistical analysis 8
Aboriginal pre-schools 11–12
Aboriginal Reconciliation 76
Aboriginal research assistants 38–39, 43
Aboriginal Research Centre (ARC)
    Commonwealth funding 62–63
    criticism from VAAL 66
    priorities 62
    publications 65
    rebranding of CRAA 57
    renamed Koorie Research Centre 68–69
    research projects 63–65
    role 63
    submissions for government agencies 65–66
    University funding 60, 63
    see also Centre for Research into Aboriginal Affairs (CRAA); Koorie Research Centre (KRC)
Aboriginal Research Centre (ARC) Board
    on special admissions scheme for Aboriginal students 57–58
    support for establishment of MOSA 85
    support for name change 69

Aboriginal Resource Centre proposal 31, 35–36, 42
Aboriginal self-determination 43
Aboriginal students
   higher education enrolments 80
   need for bridging course 61, 65
   number at Monash 61, 80, 97, 121, 128–29, 137
   in 'professional faculties' 98–99
   special entry schemes 85
   see also Monash Orientation; Monash Orientation Scheme for Aborigines (MOSA)
Aboriginal Studies
   courses in Australian institutions 31–32
   CRAA course 16, 58–60
   major and minor at Monash 70–71
   VCE teaching kit 73
   for Years 11 and 12 students 72–73
Aboriginal Studies Syllabus project 18, 19
Aboriginal Study Grants Scheme (ABSTUDY) 15, 94
Aboriginal Task Force, SAIT 90
Aboriginal and Torres Strait Islander Commission 73
Aboriginal Tutorial Assistance Scheme 127
'Aboriginal Unemployment' conference 51
'Aboriginal Wages and Employment' seminar 9–10, 29
Aboriginal women
   role models 72
   training 65
'Aborigines and the Law' seminar 38
'Aborigines and Women' subject 77
ABSCHOL 15, 26
Academic Board, Monash 74
action research 4, 8, 29
Andrews, R.R. 7
ARC see Aboriginal Research Centre (ARC)
Armidale Teachers' College 31–32
Aronson, Steve 39
Atkinson, Wayne 47, 50, 51

Austin, John 38, 74, 110–11
'Australian Aboriginal History' course 31
Australian Institute of Aboriginal Studies (AIAS) 3, 51, 55, 57
Australian Research Grants Committee (ARGC) 8
Australian Scholastic Aptitude Test 83
Australian Vice-Chancellor's Committee 15

Bandjalang Language Program 56, 63–64
Barwick (formerly McEachern), Diane 1, 9–10
Baxt, R. 84, 87
Beasley, F.R. 7
Beckett, Jeremy 1
Bell Primary School 56, 63, 64
Bernard van Leer Foundation, grant to CRAA 11–12
BHP, sponsorship of MOSA 106
Bibby, Janette 92
Bicentennial year 69–71
bilingual education programs 50
Birman, Felicia 101
'Black Australian Studies' course 31–34, 40, 49, 51–53, 58
Black, R.H. 6
Blow, Reg 54, **54**
Bnads, Helen see Curzon-Siggers, Helen
Bourke, Colin **54**
   Aboriginal committee memberships 55
   Aboriginalisation of CRAA 43–44
   AIAS sub-committee memberships 55
   background 45
   chairmanship of IAC 133
   conception of Aboriginal education 44
   as first full-time Director of CRAA 44, 46–47, 54–55
   on functions of CRAA vii
   lectures on Aboriginal education 53
   NAEC membership 45–46, 55
   on need for bridging course 60, 80, 81, 84–85

INDEX

publications   50, 58, 94
research into Aboriginal education   50
resignation   60
review of Monash's Aboriginal programs   78, 117–18, 120–24
as Supervisor of Aboriginal Education in Victoria   44
Bourke (formerly Koumalatsos), Eleanor   60, **125**
   as Aboriginal Liaison Officer at Melbourne University   52, 126
   background   126
   as Chair of Australian Indigenous Studies   125–26
   as Director of Monash Aboriginal Programs   126
   establishment of CAIS   126
   membership of CRAA Advisory Board   54, 126
   retirement   127
   review of Monash's Aboriginal programs   78, 117–18, 120–24
Bourke Report   120–24, 126
BP, sponsorship of MOSA   106
Bradley, David   81
Brailey, Jason   **136**, 138–40
Briggs, Geraldine   27
Brown, Isaac   **91, 93, 105, 107**
   background   89–90
   commitment to student welfare   103–4
   as Director of MOSA   89–91, 100, 112
   resignation   110
   on welfare fund   95
Bryant, Gordon   30–31, 35, 37
Bullivant, B.M.   68
Bureau of Aboriginal Affairs   2–4
Burke, Anna   127
Butchart, J.D.   7, 59, 83

CAIS *see* Centre for Australian Indigenous Studies (CAIS)
Campbell, Colin   8
Campbell, Sue   111, 114, 115
Carter, Wendy   49

Cattle Station Industry (NT) Award, 1951   9
Caulfield Campus   113
Cavanagh, James   38
Centre for Australian Indigenous Studies (CAIS)
   course structure and content   126–27, 134
   establishment   126
   Indigenous Student Support Unit   127, 130, 134, 135
   organisational structure   130
   review of curriculum   134–35
   see also Monash Indigenous Centre (MIC)
Centre for Continuing Education   31
Centre for Research into Aboriginal Affairs (CRAA)
   Aboriginal research assistants   38–39, 43
   Aboriginal-led and initiated research   50, 56–57
   Aboriginalisation   43–44, 46, 50, 51
   action research   4, 8, 29, 36, 37
   administrative support   6, 17
   aims and functions   vii, 5, 28, 37, 48–49, 55
   Commonwealth funding   13–14, 16, 17–21, 27, 28, 29–31, 33, 40, 42, 43, 47, 48, 56
   community education programs   36–37
   Elizabeth Eggleston Memorial Library   42, 49
   establishment   vii, 1–2, 4–7
   expansion plans of Eggleston   31–38
   funding crisis and future viability   17–21
   growth   46
   host departments   6, 17, 23
   inter-disciplinary seminars   17, 26
   library   25–26
   name changed to 'Aboriginal Research Centre'   57–58
   philanthropic support   11–12, 13
   publications   10, 26, 36, 40, 50
   as Race Relations Centre   31, 36–38

renamed vii
residential seminars 9–10
as resource centre 31, 35–36, 42, 48–49
staff 7–8, 12, 14, 23, 38–39, 47, 49
as Training Centre for Aborigines 48
University funding 6, 13, 14, 17, 18, 19, 20–21, 29, 48, 60
Victorian government funding 28, 56
see also Aboriginal Research Centre (ARC); Koorie Research Centre (KRC)
Centre for Research into Aboriginal Affairs (CRAA) Advisory Board
Aboriginal members 53–54
concerns re Black Australian Studies course 32–33
decision to appoint full-time Director 40–41
first meeting 6–7
initial composition 6
reduced to Monash staff members only 13
reservations re Studies in Aboriginal Culture proposal 34
shelving of Aboriginal Resource Centre proposal 35–36
widening of scope for proposed Race Relations Centre 37
Centre of South East Asian Studies 4
Chair of Australian Indigenous Studies, establishment 125
Chipman, Lachlan 75, 113
Chisholm Institute of Technology 112, 113
Clayton Campus 126
Clyne, Michael 67
Cochrane, Don 4, 6, 7
Coles Myer 106
Committee of Deans, Monash 19, 21, 30
Committee of Undergraduate Studies, Faculty of Arts 89
Commonwealth Conciliation and Arbitration Commission 9

Commonwealth Department of Aboriginal Affairs
funding for CRAA/ARC 30, 33, 35–36, 39, 42, 47, 48, 56, 57
funding for MOSA 88, 97, 100
withdrawal of funding for KRC 71
Commonwealth Department of Education 45, 56, 88, 97–98, 100
Commonwealth Department of Employment, Education and Training (DEET) 100, 107
Commonwealth Department of Employment and Industrial Relations 48, 65
Commonwealth Department of Prime Minister and Cabinet 12, 76
Commonwealth Tertiary Education Commission (CTEC) 98, 99, 100
Community Education Program grant 65
community education programs 36–37
consultancy service in market research 71
Coombs, H.C. 'Nugget' 12, 13
Council for Aboriginal Affairs (CAA) 12–14
CRAA *see* Centre for Research into Aboriginal Affairs (CRAA)
cultural safety training 139
Cummerragunja, history of 51, 55
Curzon-Siggers (later Bnads), Helen **107**, 125
as Director of MOSA 112, 113–14, 115–18
on Isaac Brown 103
logo for MOSA 114
as MOSA student 103, 106
resignation 125
response to Bourke Report 124

Davey, Stan 10
Davis, Gwenda 92
Davis, S.R. 7
Davison, Graeme vii–viii, 87, 94
Dawkins, J.S. 107
Department of Anthropology and Sociology 12, 17, 32

INDEX

Department of Economics 12, 17
Department of Education (Monash) 70
Department of History 94
Department of Linguistics 53
Department of Social and Preventative Medicine 39
Derham, David 7, 23, 24
Dexter, Barrie 12, 13, 18–19, 20, 21, 26, 30
Dixon, Chicka 52
Dobbin, Dr 39
Dodson, Mick 41–42
Doe, Cathy **136**
Drysdale, Marlene 123, 124
Duguid, Charles viii–ix, 5–6

Education Research and Development Committee (Cwlth) 50
Eggleston, Elizabeth **24**
   background 23
   as Director of CRAA 22–23, 24, 25–26
   expansion plans for CRAA 31–38
   and Group for Information on Aboriginal Affairs 39–40
   illness and death 23, 26, 41
   initial involvement at CRAA 7–8, 12
   as lecturer in Law Faculty 23
   legacy 41–42
   legal services for Aboriginal people 8, 27
   personality and temperament 24–25
   PhD research 7, 25
   as public intellectual 26
Eggleston Foundation viii
Eggleston, *Sir* Richard 23, 45, 110
Elizabeth Eggleston Fund 95
Elizabeth Eggleston Memorial Aboriginal Resource Centre 42, 49
Elizabeth Eggleston Memorial Library 42, 49, 127
Elizabeth Eggleston Trust 72
Engel, *Rev* Frank 6
Estcourt, Angela **136**
Experience Monash Day 137

Faculty of Arts 59–60, 83, 86, 89, 125, 126
Faculty of Economics and Politics (ECPOS) 12, 95–96
Faculty of Education 83
Faculty of Law 23, 83, 86, 98
Faculty of Medicine 8
Federal Council for the Advancement of Aboriginal and Torres Strait Islanders 10, 30
Ferntree Gully Women's Educational Cooperative 53
Fesl, Eve **67, 107**
   on Aboriginal education 70
   as Acting Director of ARC 61, 62
   as Acting Director of MOSA 74–75, 111, 113
   background 61–62
   Bandjalang Language Project 56, 63–64
   on Bicentenary 69
   as Director of ARC/KRC 61, 63, 75
   doctoral dissertation 67
   employment in CRAA 58, 61
   and establishment of MOSA 65, 80, 84, 85, 87
   legal proceedings against VAAL 66
   as Member of the Order of Austalia 69
   personality and temperament 62, 66–67
   public education classes in Aboriginal Studies 53
   public profile 72
   research 51
   research interests 63
   resignation from Monash 75, 113
   suggests ARC be renamed Koorie Research Centre 68
   as tutor for Aboriginal Studies course 58
   as Victorian of the Year 72
Firebrace, Sharon 66, 76–78
Fletcher-Kennedy, Helen vii, viii, 131, 133–34, 135, 136, 138
Foley, Gary 111

Frankston Campus   113
'Future of the South-Eastern Australian Aborigines' conference   51
Gallery Building, Clayton Campus   71, 74, 101, **102**, 135
Gilbert, Kevin   47
Gippsland Campus   126
Gippsland Centre for Koori Studies (GCKS)   74, 78, 112, 113, 121, 122, 124, 126
Gippsland Institute of Advance Education   74, 112
Gott, Beth   133
Grassby, Al   37
Grey, Lex   12
Griffith University   75
Group of Eight (Go8), Indigenous Access ranking   129, 130
Group for Information on Aboriginal Affairs   39
Groves, Bert   10
Gruen, Fred   9

Hand, Gerry   **102**, 107
'Hands On Monash Camp'   136, 137
Hank Young Trust – Koorie Welfare and Education Reference Board   73, 107
Hawke, Robert (Bob)   97
Helen M. Schutt Trust   95
Heraud, Phil   101
Herbert Vere Evatt Memorial Foundation   95
Hetzel, Basil   20, 27, 28, 41, 46
Higher Education Equity Program (Cwlth)   109
Higher Education Research Unit, Monash   33
Hill, Fiona   92
Hirst, John   31
Howson, Peter   28
Hughes, Paul   108
Hyatt, Rob   101, 102, 104

Indigenous Access and Support Programs Task Force, Monash   129, 130
Indigenous Advisory Council (IAC)   133, 135

Indigenous Enabling Program (IEP)   137–39
Indigenous Engagement Unit   135
Indigenous Strategic Framework   139
Indigenous Student Support Unit   127, 130, 134, 135
Indigenous Welcome Day   132
inter-disciplinary seminars   17, 26

Jackomos, Merle   27
Jackson, Daryl   71
James, Margaret   124
Jameson, Richard   109
Jesus, as speaker of English   viii
Johnson, Colin (aka Mudrooroo Narogin)   47, 50, 55, 58, 94
Jordan, Deirdre   100

Keleher, Kerrie   94
Keleher, Kristel   **136**
Kendall, Carol   104
Knight, Noretta   47
Knox, Bruce   68–69, 124
Koori Kollij   70, 88–89
'Koori'/'Koorie', use of word   68
Koorie Advisory Committee   123
Koorie Institute for Research, Development and Education   123
Koorie Research Centre (KRC)
   Aboriginal Studies program for VCE teachers   73
   Aboriginal Studies teaching kit   73
   Bourke Report recommendations   122
   Bourke review   120
   consultancy service in market research   71
   disestablishment   126
   financial situation   72, 73–74, 75
   loss of Commonwealth funding   71–72
   name changed from ARC   68–69
   premises   71, 74
   private donations   72, 73
   research and publications   78, 122
   review   75–76
   see also Aboriginal Research Centre

INDEX

(ARC); Centre for Research into Aboriginal Affairs (CRAA)
Koumalatsos, Eleanor *see* Bourke (formerly Koumalatsos), Eleanor
KRC *see* Koorie Research Centre (KRC)

La Trobe University 31
Lance Reichstein Charitable Foundation 95
Langman, Ian 15
Langton, Marcia 52
Leading the Way: The Monash Plan 1998–2002 123
legal aid system for Aboriginal people in Victoria 8, 27
Legge, J.D. 4, 53, 59, 87
Lilley, Ian 134–35
Lincoln Institute of Health Sciences 90
Link-Up 69
Lippman, Lorna 12, 14, 23, 30, 33, 41
Logan, Mal **67**, 70, **74**
Lordbja Victorian Language Centre 73
Lush, *Sir* George 66

McEachern, Diane *see* Barwick (formerly McEachern), Diane
McGinness, Joseph 6, 10
McGuiness, Bruce 26, 34, 39, 40, 52, 70
Mackay, Michael 78
McLean, Sue *see* Stevenson (formerly McLean), Sue
McNamee, Brian 92
McNamee, Robin **107**
Maori Education Fellowship 12
Marist College 51
Markus, Andrew 94, 116, 125
Marshall, A.J. 7
Marshall, Peter 124
Martin, Carolin 47
Martin, Gary 92, **93**
Martin, Ray **54**, 98
Marwick, M.G. 7
Matheson, J.A.L. 3, 4, 13, 14, 15, 16, 19–20, 21
Maxwell, Penny 54
Maza, Bob 34
Meagher E.R. 27

Menzies Building 42, 94, 102, 135
Merritt, Robert (Bobby) 56, 57
MIC *see* Monash Indigenous Centre
Milingimbi artists and performers 51
Monash Act 2009 132
Monash College 130, 137, 138
Monash Indigenous Centre (MIC) vii, 135, 140–41
Monash Orientation Scheme for Aborigines (MOSA)
  Aboriginal support for 84–85
  assessment structures 96–97
  Austin's suspension as Directorship 111
  Bourke Report recommendations 120–22
  business management stream 115
  community outreach program 116–17
  corporate sponsors 106
  cost of program 110
  course structure and content 92–94, 115, 122
  criticisms aired on *7.30 Report* 114
  Director's position 89
  encouraging pride in Aboriginal culture and identity 93–94, 102–3
  establishment vii, 61, 65
  funding arrangements 88, 97–98, 100, 105–7
  humanities stream 115, 116
  impact on enrolments 80
  impact on students 94, 97, 101, 102–3, 118
  implementation of scheme 87–88
  independent external review 100, 104
  line-management support for Director 112
  logo 114
  as model other institutions 80–81
  premises 74, 101–2
  private donations 106–7
  proposal for 81–87
  rebranding 114
  Recruitment Officer position 109
  as resource centre 117

– 155 –

review 78
role of director 75
scholarships 106
science stream 98–100, 101, 115
selection of students 90–92, 104, 111–12, 116
staff 90, 94, 100, 101, 104, 118, 121
stipends and welfare fund 94–95, 105–7
student numbers 95, 109–10, 111, 115–16, 118, 121
student success rate 97, 110, 115
suspension and disbanding of program 118, 122
Monash University
Aboriginal Education Strategy Plan 112–13
Aboriginal employment strategy 123, 124
academic standards 83
archives viii–ix
Council resolution re Indigenous Australians 131
ethos 4
Go8 ranking for Indigenous Access 129
Indigenous initiatives 131–32
Indigenous programs as University-wide priority 120
Indigenous student enrolments 61, 80, 97, 121, 128, 137
internationalisation of curriculum 123
recruitment of Indigenous students 129–30
reputation 86
Moriarty, John 10
MOSA *see* Monash Orientation Scheme for Aborigines (MOSA)
MOSA Committee 87–88, 90
MOSA shop 117
Murray, Gary 38
Murray, Stewart 27
Myer 28

NAIDOC Week 132
National Aboriginal Education Committee (NAEC) 45–46, 55, 84
National Aboriginal Employment Development Committee 51, 55
National Aboriginal and Torres Strait Islander Education Policy 109, 112
national apology to Australia's Indigenous people 130
National Employment Strategy for Aborigines 48
National and Employment Training (NEAT) scheme 48
National Sorry Day 132
National Union of Australian University Students 15
Nelson later Reed, Elizabeth 95, 104, 110, 111
Newfong, John 52
Newsletter on Aboriginal Affairs 39–40
Newton, Janice 90, 91–92, 94, 104
Nona, Barbara 92
North Australian Workers Union 9
Northern Territory University 110
Nura Gili 130

O'Donoghue, Lois 52
Office of Aboriginal Affairs (OAA) 12, 16, 17–21, 29–30
Onus, Austin 39
Onus, Lin 39

Page, Juanita 90, 111
Palm River 76
Pearce, Trevor 106
Perkins, Charles 10, 52
'Personal Development Through Literacy' project 64–65
Potts, Daniel 94
Preston Technical School 64
Professorial Board, Monash 4, 6, 15, 68, 86, 87

Quartly, Marian 94, 124

Race and Ethnic Relations Centre 37
Rachinger, W.A. 86
racism viii, 70
Read, Peter 69

INDEX

Reconciliation Action Plan (RAP) 139
Reed (formerly Nelson), Elizabeth 104, 110, 111
referendum, 1967 12
Renkin, P.F. 35–36, 40
Ricklefs, Merle 65, 74, **74**, **107**
   appeal to PM to save MOSA 97–98
   background x, 81
   as Chair of MOSA Committee 87–88, 90, 94–95
   establishment of MOSA 60, 61, 80, 87–88
   as Head of Aboriginal Programs 74, 112–13
   on MOSA's assessment structures 96
   on national role of MOSA 99
   proposal for MOSA 81–84
   resignation from Monash 113
Risdale, Angela 95, 104
Roach, Archie 38
Roach, Austin 38
Robertson, Peter 106
Robinson, David 78, 120, 123, 129
Robinvale Primary School 64
Roper, Tom 71
Rothfield, Norman 72
Rowley, Charles 3, 6, 9, 26, 41
Royal Commission into Aboriginal Deaths in Custody (RCADIC) 77, 78
Rudd, Kevin 130
Russell, Lynette vii, 127–28, 130, 134, 135, 140–41

Scott, W.H. 81
Secondary Schools Aboriginal Fund (Vic) 28
'Seminar on Studies in Aboriginal Culture' 34
7.30 Report (ABC television) 114
Shoemaker, Adam 131, 135
Silberauer, George 75, 76
Sinclair, W.A. 96
Singh, Aunty Diane 136, **136**
Smallcombe, Sonia 112
Smith, George Warwick 6
Social Science Research Council (SSRC) Aborigines Project 3, 9

South African Institute of Race Relations 2–3, 36
South Australian Institute of Technology (SAIT) 85, 86, 90
Spalding, Ian 10
Stanner, W.E.H. 12
Stevens, Frank 26
Stevenson (formerly McLean), Sue 7, 12, 23, 24
stolen generations 69
'Studies in Aboriginal Culture' proposal 31, 34–35
Swan, J.M. 87
Swift, M.G. 14, 16, 17, 18

Tatz, Colin **5**
   Aboriginal Studies course at Armidale 31–32
   appointment at Monash 2
   appointment at University of New England 15, 19, 20
   attempts tof secure government funding for CRRA 13–14, 16, 18–21
   background x, 2
   as Director of CRAA 7
   establishment of CRAA 1–2
   as executive officer of CRAA and Advisory Board 7
   on 'how far we've come' 142–43
   library 25
   membership of Aborigines Welfare Board 8–9, 11
   as mentor to Elizabeth Eggleston 7, 23
   offer of Chair at Waikato 15
   personality and temperament 2, 4, 16, 18, 20, 21, 24
   proposed 'Bureau of Aboriginal Affairs' 2–4
   as provisional secretary of CRAA and Advisory Board 6, 7
   research initiatives 8–9, 19
   sabbaticals 13
   view of AIAS 3, 55
Telecom Australia 73, 106
Thorpe, Steve 39

Tonkinson, Robert 66
Torres Strait Islander flag 132
Tranby Aboriginal College 88
Turner, Ian 7

Ucko, Peter 55
University of Melbourne 52, 83, 86
University of New South Wales 85, 129–30
University of Sydney 129

Valadian, Margaret 52
Victorian Aboriginal Child Care Agency 56–57
Victorian Aboriginal Cooperative 56, 57
Victorian Aboriginal Educational Consultative Group 55, 56, 63, 85
Victorian Aboriginal Legal Service 27
Victorian Aborigines Advancement League (VAAL) 8, 27, 30, 51, 56, 66
Victorian Aborigines Welfare Board 8, 27
Victorian Council for Aboriginal Culture 34–35
Victorian Council of Churches 39
Victorian Council of Social Services 51
Victorian Department of Aboriginal Affairs 28
Victorian Department of Community Welfare 56
Victorian Department of Education 44, 45, 50, 51, 56, 72–73
Victorian Department of Health 8, 40
Victorian Health Commission 90
Victorian In-Service Education Committee Aboriginal Sub-Committee 55
Viner, Ian **54**

Walker, Brian **136**
Walker, Kath 10, 52
Waller, Louis x, 8, 23, 25, 27, 41, 46, 53, **54**
Walpiri language 64
Warrnambool West Primary School 56, 63, 64

welfare services for Victorian Aboriginal people 51
Wentworth, W.C. (Bill) 15–16, 19, 20, 21
Wesley College 73
Western Australian Institute of Technology (WAIT) 85, 86, 90
White, Isobel 58, 94
'white–Aboriginal relations in Riverina' project 18
Whitlam government 30, 36, 43
William Buckland Foundation 95
Willmot, Eric 44–45, 60
Winslow, Laura 39, 40
Wurreker Award for University Pathways 136

Young, Hank 106–7
Yulendj Indigenous Engagement Unit vii, 130, 135–40
Yunupingu, Galarrwuy 52